6.00
2

W9-AMT-593

ETHICS AND WORLD POLITICS:
FOUR PERSPECTIVES

Studies in International Affairs Number 18

Studies in International Affairs Number 18

ETHICS AND WORLD POLITICS:
FOUR PERSPECTIVES

Ernest W. Lefever, Editor

Mark O. Hatfield

Paul Ramsey

Arthur Schlesinger, Jr.

The Washington Center of Foreign Policy Research
School of Advanced International Studies
The Johns Hopkins University

The Johns Hopkins University Press, Baltimore and London

The chapter by Arthur Schlesinger, Jr., "National Interests and Moral Absolutes," is reprinted from the August 1971 issue of *Harper's Magazine* by permission of the author. Copyright © 1971 by Minneapolis Star and Tribune Co., Inc.

Manufactured in the United States of America

The Johns Hopkins University Press, Baltimore, Maryland 21218
The Johns Hopkins University Press Ltd., London

Library of Congress Catalog Card Number 75-186511
ISBN 0-8018-1395-6 (clothbound edition)
ISBN 0-8018-1400-6 (paperbound edition)

Library of Congress Cataloging in Publication Data will be found on the last printed page of this book.

In Appreciation

We at the Johns Hopkins School of Advance International Studies affectionately dedicate this volume to *Mrs. George Hyman* of Washington, D. C., whose keen interest in world affairs and whose generous assistance to the School have made possible the Christian A. Herter Lecture Series.

PREFACE

For nearly a decade the Christian A. Herter Lecture Series has been an integral part of the program of the Johns Hopkins School of Advanced International Studies. In 1964 the faculty established the series to honor the distinguished American who had founded the School some twenty years earlier. It was the hope of the faculty that our lecture platform in Washington might be used by highly qualified individuals to present different points of view about international relations and to examine in depth some of the basic issues that confront the United States in a rapidly changing world.

In this hope we have not been disappointed. Many distinguished people have lectured in the Herter series. Moreover, a number of provocative books—including Barbara Ward's *The Lopsided World,* J. William Fulbright's *The Arrogance of Power,* and Gunnar Myrdahl's *The Poverty of Nations*—have emerged as a direct result of the lectures.

In 1971 the Herter lectures broke new ground, largely in response to student interest in using them to deal explicitly with the normative aspects for foreign policy and in having several points of view expressed. As a result, we decided to have three distinguished Americans address the topic, "Morality and International Politics." Each lecturer was asked to respond in his own way to the following questions:

1. What is the historic role of moral values in international politics? Is there any necessary contradiction between Western ethical values and the pursuit of the "national interest"?

2. Have modern weapons, technology, communications, social developments, or other international and domestic factors changed the actual or possible role of moral values in relations between states? Is the existing interstate system obsolete?

3. Under what circumstances is the state justified in using military force beyond its borders? Is the armed support of revolution or opposition to revolution in other countries ever justifiable?

4. What are the prospects for peaceful change toward greater justice and security among states?

To insure diversity in perspective, the three men selected for the lectures were a historian, a theologian, and a statesman:

Dr. Arthur Schlesinger, Jr., Albert Schweitzer Professor in the Humanities, City University of New York and author of *The Vital Center* (1949), *The Politics of Upheaval* (1960), *A Thousand Days: John F. Kennedy in the White House* (1965), and many other books and essays.

Dr. Paul Ramsey, Harrington Spear Pain Professor of Religion at Princeton University and author of *Basic Christian Ethics* (1950), *Nine Modern Moralists* (1962), *The Just War* (1968), and other books.

Senator Mark O. Hatfield, Republican from Oregon, former Governor of Oregon and Associate Professor of Political Science at Willamette University.

From the outset of the planning, we enlisted the services of Dr. Ernest W. Lefever to set up the lectures and to edit the book we hoped would come out of them. Dr. Lefever, who is a recognized authority on morality and foreign policy, has also contributed a fourth perspective to the volume. He is a Senior Fellow in Foreign Policy Studies at the Brookings Institution and a member of the recently constituted Johns Hopkins Society of Scholars. Among the books he has written or edited are *Ethics and United States Foreign Policy* (1957), *Arms and Arms Control* (1962), and *Uncertain Mandate: Politics of the U.N. Congo Operation* (1967). A selected bibliography of readily available titles that bear on morality and international politics, prepared by Mr. Lefever, is included in the present volume.

The subject of morality and international politics is fascinating, and I cannot resist the temptation to comment briefly on two or three of the issues raised in the chapters that follow.

Let me say at the outset that most of us have great difficulty identifying the moral issues in the field of foreign relations and even greater difficulty determining what should be done about them, regardless of whether we have strong religious convictions or whether we take a hard or soft line toward the Soviet Union and the Cold War differences that divide the East and the West. Certainly moral considerations, consciously or unconsciously, affect the thinking of most Americans about such problems as disarmament, colonialism, the Vietnam war, foreign aid, the anti-ballistic missile, NATO, and the continuing Middle East crisis. But moral issues rarely stand out in bold relief; they are often obscured by other factors to which we may attach greater importance.

The kind of dilemma which confronts all of us was pointed up in dramatic fashion at the height of the Cuban missile crisis. Was it "morally wrong" for President Kennedy to run the grave risks of a nuclear war—with the potential tremendous loss of human lives that such a course implies—in order to do what he thought was necessary to meet the Soviet challenge in Cuba? Did the end justify the means? Or is it possible that the threat of nuclear war would have been considerably greater at some later stage if the President had used less forceful means and failed to oust Soviet offensive weapons from Cuban soil? Many Americans who shared the same moral convictions about war, the preservation of human life, and the desirability of settling disputes by peaceful means found themselves on different sides of this issue.

Looking at American foreign policy in this light should make us more appreciative of those who are charged with the awful responsibility for making the fateful decisions of war and peace. American policy—partly because of our role of leadership in the world—at best is a series of extremely difficult choices. By the very nature of things, most really important decisions are difficult; normally they don't reach the president's desk unless they are difficult. They are not simple choices between good and bad, or black and white, or right and wrong; they are usually very tough and unhappy choices between two or more less than desirable courses of action.

The average citizen, unhampered by official responsibilities, may make up his mind on whether to recognize the People's Republic of China, stop nuclear tests, withdraw from foreign military bases, or sell jet fighter planes to Israel, without worrying very much about public opinion, the rules of international law, the military consequences, the attitude of the nonaligned countries, the role of Congress, the position of our allies, the national budget, humanitarian considerations, or the impact of such actions upon our position in the world. But the president and the secretary of state cannot act in a vacuum. They must consider all the important factors involved including the moral issues.

As Dr. Kenneth W. Thompson reminds us, "Men act in diplomacy because they must, their choices are hedged about, and the ground on which they stand seldom is wholly of their own choosing." As a result our country sometimes finds itself saddled with bad policies, not because our policy-makers are inept, or their motives wrong, or their ideals warped, or because they lack an understanding of ethics in world affairs, but because the range of practical choices with which they are faced makes a "good" decision virtually impossible.

In this connection let me say just a few words about style, for in world affairs the *conduct* of foreign policy may be almost as important as its *substance*. I am not suggesting that good manners can serve as a substitute for morals or for a sound policy. But the methods we use and the procedures we follow may, in some cases, be as important as the policy itself.

Here interested citizens are in an excellent position to make a valuable contribution to our foreign policy. Is our government honest and sincere in its dealing with others? Do we respect the attitudes and the interests of other peoples and other nations? Is our behavior in world affairs characterized by high moral standards? The objectives of our policy may sometimes be obscure or in dispute, but our people have every right to insist that the methods our government uses in reaching its goals should meet those standards of honesty and morality that decent men might expect from the leader of the free world.

No one can doubt that this kind of behavior pays off in foreign relations just as it does in every day life. I have often seen delegates to international conferences engender ill-will and distrust by their rigidity, their violent language and their unwillingness to behave as reasonable men should. Perhaps the most dramatic example was in 1960 when Chairman Khrushchev broke up the U.N. General Assembly meeting by pounding his shoe on the table of the Russian delegation. As one of the principals in that historic event, I can certify that his rudeness did not win any friends to the Communist cause. Quite the contrary. Many delegates were shocked and saddened by his open defiance of normal parliamentary procedures and his disregard for the rights of others. It is well to remember that even good policies can be drained of their content by bad manners, deceit and petty conduct.

This suggests that our diplomats should conduct their negotiations not only with a good deal of firmness and realism, but also with an infinite amount of patience, a willingness to accept reasonable compromise, an honest reluctance to engage in Cold War invective, and a desire to explore every honorable avenue of accommodation. At the same time they should exert every effort to uncover new and promising alternatives rather than adopt a rigid, negative posture which holds no hope for the future. America shares certain common interests with Russia and China and we must do our utmost to enlarge the area of agreement where we can.

Gladstone once remarked that the task of statesmanship is to discover the direction God Almighty is going to take during the next fifty years and act accordingly. I would not contend that the authors of this little book have any "inside" information to give us on this point. Nevertheless, their topic is an important one, and if their contributions stimulate further discussion of ethics and world politics—as I am sure they will—the book will serve a very useful purpose.

FRANCIS O. WILCOX, Dean
Johns Hopkins School of Advanced
International Studies

CONTENTS

ETHICS AND WORLD POLITICS:
FOUR PERSPECTIVES

I. MORALITY VERSUS MORALISM IN FOREIGN POLICY

Ernest W. Lefever

The rising moral concern among Americans in the late 1960s about the conduct and consequences of their government's foreign policy has often been accompanied by increased moral confusion and impassioned rhetoric. Moral and political perplexity is not without merit, because the uncertainty it betokens can sometimes lead to greater understanding and more responsible behavior. The deterioration of moral discourse, not confined to critics or supporters of any particular foreign policy, is the product of recent external developments and a persistent philosophical ambiguity in the American character.

It is too simple to attribute the pervasive moral confusion to American involvement in Vietnam, though that protracted trauma doubtless has brought to a head the growing weariness with the burdens of our power and the disenchantment with what Denis Brogan once called "the illusion of American omnipotence." Even before Vietnam our earlier and more naive national self-confidence had been shattered by a series of disappointments and reverses—the "fall of China" in 1949, the inconclusive Korean war, the loss of Cuba to the Communist camp, and the divisiveness, conflict, and war that have followed in the wake of decolonization. With these bitter lessons, most Americans have finally learned

The author wishes to express appreciation to Robert A. Gessert for his helpful criticism of this essay.

1

that even the mighty United States cannot shape the destiny of peoples in the larger world, at least not without violating our profound moral inhibitions against the exercise of unabashed force to aggrandize our power or nourish our vanity. Few spokesmen since Pearl Harbor, other than Henry Luce, have advocated that we shed our cherished scruples in the quest for an American imperium.

Underlying the moral awakening and confusion has been a continuing struggle between two different ways of looking at history and politics, two streams of American thought that have vied for ascendency, especially since the mid-nineteenth century. I refer to what the late Reinhold Niebuhr has called "rational idealism" and "historical realism," each manifesting itself in diverging political attitudes, expectations, and behavior.

Rational idealism in essence is the child of the Enlightenment and Social Darwinism, and in its pure form it affirms the perfectability, or at least improvability, of man and the possibility, if not inevitability, of progress in history. The diverse schools within this approach are united in their ultimate faith in the nobler nature of man. The earlier idealists saw reason as the redemptive agent that would save man and politics and eventually inaugurate an era of universal peace and brotherhood—the socialist paradise or the Kingdom of God on earth. The natural goodness of man, they believed, could be translated into the structures of politics. Poverty, injustice, and war could be eliminated. The rational idealists were supported by the views of men such as Tom Paine, Walt Whitman, and Walter Rauschenbusch, the articulate spokesman of the Protestant Social Gospel movement. Wilsonian idealism, the manifestation of rationalism in the international sphere, reached its zenith in 1928 with the signing of the Kellogg-Briand

Pact outlawing war as an "instrument of national policy."

Historical realism, in contrast, emphasizes the moral limits of human nature and history and has its roots in St. Augustine, John Calvin, Edmund Burke, James Madison, and most other classical Western thinkers. Rejecting all forms of religious and secular utopianism—including fascism and communism—the post-Versailles realists have included men as varied as Reinhold Niebuhr, Carl L. Becker, Winston Churchill, and Dean Acheson. Noting that the extravagant expectations of the Wilsonians were not ratified by subsequent events, the self-designated realists hold that all political achievements are limited by man's dogged resistance to drastic reconstruction. With this recognition of "original sin," they argue that perfect peace, justice, security, and freedom are not possible in this world, though approximations of these lofty goals are not beyond man's grasp. To the rational idealist, the "impossible ideal" is achievable because it is rationally conceivable. To the historical realist, the "impossible ideal" is relevant because it lends humility without despair and hope without illusion.

There are few wholly consistent adherents to either approach. Were Jefferson and Lincoln rational idealists or historical realists? Obviously they were a combination of both: Jefferson leaning toward the idealistic view and Lincoln toward the realistic. Like most Americans, they tended to be optimistic about the more distant future and at the same time practical and realistic about immediate problems and possibilities.

Rational idealism and historical realism are not complete moral systems but two different perspectives coexisting uneasily within the Western commitment to a political order of justice and freedom. As approaches, they are subject to certain limitations and weaknesses. In one sense each tends to balance and correct the other.

Most moral philosophers, political theorists, and states-men tend toward one view or the other. On the practical level, virtually all political leaders have been realists, regardless of how idealistic their rhetoric may have been. While I believe that the historical realist approach is a more adequate reading of the deepest Judaeo-Christian tradition and a sounder guide to the art of politics than its post-Enlightenment rival, I recognize that it, like rational idealism, is subject to corruption.

Both of these respectable philosophical approaches have in fact been demeaned and distorted by emphasizing certain of their virtues to the neglect or exclusion of other elements in the larger body of Western normative thought. Each is vulnerable in its own way to the vices of political aloofness, on the one hand, and crusading arrogance, on the other. Rational idealists, frustrated by stubborn political realities, sometimes degenerate into sentimentalists whose strident demand for perfection becomes a substitute for responsible behavior. When personal purity becomes more important than political effectiveness, the resulting aloofness is virtually indistin-guishable from that of the Machiavellians who cynically insist that might alone makes right. The historical realist becomes irresponsible when his preoccupation with man's baser nature cuts the taproot of social concern and permits him to become a defender of injustice or tyranny.

A lopsided realist can come to hold that what is good for America is good for the rest of the world and that it is our "manifest destiny" to make other peoples over in our own image, by force if necessary. An equally lopsided idealist can support efforts to reshape other societies by more subtle, but not necessarily less reprehensible, means. Members of each approach can degenerate into cynical isolationists or overbearing crusaders. Seen in this light, the extremists in both groups really have more in common with each other than with the mainstream of their own tradition.

The corruption of realism or idealism can be called *moralism*—the most popular rival and impostor of genuine *morality*. Morality or ethics (the Greek derivative with the same meaning) has to do with right or wrong behavior in all spheres. It is a discipline of ends and means. However primitive or sophisticated, all moral systems define normative ends and acceptable rules for achieving them. Moralism, on the other hand, is a sham morality, a partial ethic. Often it is expressed in self-righteous rhetoric or manipulative symbols designed to justify, enlist, condemn, or deceive rather than to inform, inspire, or serve the cause of justice. The moralism of the naive and well-intentioned may be sincere. The moralism of the ambitious and sophisticated is likely to be dishonest. Intellectually flabby and morally undisciplined, moralism tends to focus on private interests rather than the public good, on the immediate at the expense of the future, and on sentiment rather than reason. It is often more concerned with appearances than consequences. Morality is a synonym for responsibility and moralism is a conscious or unconscious escape from accountability.

The varieties of moralism flowing from the corruption of the two approaches always subvert honest political dialogue and responsible behavior, but at the present point in American history *soft moralism* of the sentimental idealists is a greater threat than *hard moralism* of the power realists. The views of the hard cynics—the Machiavellis and imperialists—find little hospitality in the university, the church, the mass press, or in the public generally. Few Americans call for the reconquest of the Philippines or the "liberation" of Cuba or Eastern

Europe. The small voice of the hard moralists is barely audible. In sharp contrast, the soft moralism of the rational idealists has had increasing appeal because many Americans are wearied by the burdens of power—the cost of nuclear deterrence and the perplexities of helping to keep the peace in distant places.

Today the rational idealistic approach—in its religious and secular versions— and the various corruptions of this stance find wide acceptance in the church and university and are actively promoted by the mass media. Given the high level of moral turbulence and uncertainty, it is important to take critical note of this more pervasive manifestation of American moralism, acknowledging that some of its attributes are also similar to those of hard moralism.

*   *   *

Moralism, soft or hard, tends toward a single-factor approach to political problems, while mainstream Western morality emphasizes multiple causation, multiple ends, and multiple responsibilities. Many Americans have demanded peace (often simplistically defined as the absence of war), with insufficient regard for the other two great social ends—justice and freedom. Some have urged the United States to withdraw immediately and totally from Vietnam or to stop building nuclear arms without weighing the probable impact of their advice on the prospects for justice in Southeast Asia, freedom in Western Europe, or global stability. Others have insisted that U.S. involvement in the Third World has thwarted the march toward justice. If one of several valued goals—peace, justice, or freedom—becomes the supreme political end, the other two are bound to suffer. Peace (order) without justice and freedom is tyranny. Justice without freedom is another form of tyranny.

The statesman has a multiple mandate to use the resources at his command to maintain a tolerable balance among the competing claims of order, justice, and freedom, though in grave crises he may be compelled to sacrifice one temporarily to save the other two. Confronted with the infamy of Pearl Harbor, the American people sacrificed peace in the interests of security and were prepared to accept limitations on their freedom for the same end. Any political community must enjoy minimal security before it can develop the discipline of justice and the safeguards of freedom.

The preoccupation with one particular value, such as "the right of self-determination (one expression of freedom), undercuts wise statesmanship and often has dire consequences. The single-minded emphasis on self-determination insured the Balkanization of Eastern Europe after World War I. In the 1960s when the Katanga and Biafra lobbies marched under the same banner of self-determination the result was prolonged conflict and suffering in the abortive secessionist attempts in the Congo (Zaire) and Nigeria. The pro-Biafra crusade, a dramatic example of the moral flabbiness of single-issue causes, was an improbable conglomeration of the New Left and old right, humanitarians and hirelings, churchmen and secularists, isolationists and interventionists.

*　　　*　　　*

The soft moralistic view tends to distrust the state, especially its coercive power, while Western ethical thought affirms the necessity of the state and insists on the responsible use of its power. Absolute power may corrupt absolutely, as Lord Acton asserted, but less-than-absolute power may or may not corrupt those who exercise it. There is little evidence that Lincoln, Churchill, or Truman were corrupted by power; they may even have been ennobled by it. Hitler, Stalin, and Mao were doubtless corrupted before they gained power. Power is amoral. It can be enlisted to liberate or enslave, to guarantee security or take it away. There is a vast difference between the Germany of Adolf Hitler and the Germany of Willy Brandt.

The state government must possess a monopoly on the legitimate use of violence within its domain. As the sovereign authority over a given territory—whether city, country, or empire—the government is the ultimate agency for resolving internal conflicts of power and interest. Were it not for the state, Saint Augustine said, men would devour one another as fishes. Martin Luther said the central task of the state was to protect the innocent by restraining evil men. Of the modern democratic state, Professor Niebuhr said: "Man's capacity for justice makes democracy possible; but man's inclination to injustice makes democracy necessary."[1] The problem is not to eliminate the state, the professed goal of Marxists and anarchists alike, but to make political power accountable to its citizens by a system that permits them peaceably to give or withhold consent and if necessary to throw the rascals out. If a government becomes tyrannical and all peaceful means for redressing grievances have been exhausted, the people, said Lincoln, have the right to rebel by violent means. The acceptance of Lincoln's view on the right of revolution does not negate the essential character of the responsible state. It is the fundamental agency for "insuring domestic tranquility, providing for the common defense, promoting the general welfare, and

---

[1] Reinhold Niebuhr, *The Children of Light and the Children of Darkness* (New York: Charles Scribner's Sons, 1944), p. xi.

securing the blessings of liberty." In serving these central social objectives there is no substitute for the state—the sovereign political community.

*   *   *

Soft moralism is highly critical of the exercise of American military power, except in self-defense and this is often narrowly defined. America has been criticized for throwing its weight around, and even for repressive policies toward the Third World, though solid evidence is seldom adduced to buttress these charges. On the other hand, a few hard zealots have called for a stronger exercise of power to impose an American order in one part of the world or the other. Classical moralists reject both the arbitrary abstention from power and its unrestrained use and insist that the United States has a responsibility for international peace and order commensurate with its capacity to affect external events. Our military power—as a deterrent, a threat, or an active force—should be limited to dealing with real and present dangers to world peace. A workable international order can rest only on a propitious balance of forces with each of the two superpowers inescapably playing a vital role. U.S. military might, including its nuclear arsenal, is an essential factor in preventing a shift in the balance of forces that could lead to war or the capitulation of friendly states to nuclear blackmail.

The international security system led by the United States—involving NATO, other mutual defense arrangements, and military assistance—has gone a long way to protect the weak against the ambitions of the strong. What would have been the fate of Western Europe, Greece, Turkey, Iran, Thailand, Taiwan, South Korea, and Japan if the United States had not extended its protection? Since the balance sheet on Southeast Asia is not yet completed, it is not certain that U.S. involvement has set back the long-range prospects for stability, order, and freedom. American security assistance to some fifty Third World states in the past two decades has helped to maintain in many of them that minimal stability essential to constructive political and economic development.

To affirm an indispensable American responsibility for reinforcing the chance for peaceful change is not to define the specific disciplines of that role. How, when, and under what circumstances Washington should threaten or use how much coercion—this perplexing political and moral question—can be resolved only by statesmen who understand both the limits and possibilities of American power in situations where the United States has little control and an uncertain moral mandate. Because of these complexities and uncertainty about its own responsibilities, the United States has on occasion used too little or too much power or exercised it too early or too late. The Bay of Pigs comes to mind.

*   *   *

Some adherents of the moralistic approach advocate interventionist foreign policies designed to reshape the internal customs and institutions of other states. At the same time, they often downgrade or even deprecate the primary security role of foreign policy. This strange combination of reform-intervention and security-isolation turns foreign policy on its head. In the classical view, the first task of external policy is peace and security, and the first task of domestic policy is order and justice. The reform-interventionists, soft or hard, blur the salient distinction between what can and ought to be done by a government for its own people, and what can and ought to to be done by a government in the vast external realm over which it has no legal jurisdiction and where its moral and political mandate is severely limited. The insistence that the U.S. government employ extraordinary and sometimes coercive means to reshape the internal political, economic, or social structures in other sovereign communities is morally arrogant and flies in the face of the most basic international law which, in the words of the U.N. Charter, prohibits intervention "in matters which are essentially within the domestic jurisdiction of any state."

Western morality respects the right of each political community to develop in its own way at its own pace, as long as it does not impinge coercively on other political communities. President Nixon's words in Rumania in 1969 were a refreshing restatement of this principle: "We seek normal relations with all countries, regardless of their domestic systems"; each state has the right to "preserve its national institutions." His trip to China underscored his words. Ignoring this self-constraint, moralistic voices keep urging the U.S. government to withhold security or economic aid to force domestic changes within Brazil, Greece, and other friendly states whose structure or policies do not accord with the critic's preferences.

This peculiar American penchant to export our virtue reached a high-water mark, at least in rhetoric, under President Kennedy and found belated legislative sanction in 1966 in Title IX of the Foreign Assistance Act which declared that all U.S. economic aid programs should encourage the development of "democratic private and local governmental institutions" in the recipient countries by using their "intellectual resources" to stimulate "economic and social progress" and by supporting "civic education and training skills required for effective participation in governmental and political processes essential to self-goverment." This intrusive sally into other people's affairs, however naive or wrongheaded, does not compare to the breathtaking sweep or moral pretension of the Communist Manifesto with its strident call to the workers of the world (read "self-appointed elect") to redeem societies everywhere without regard to state frontiers. Arrogance is the chief sin. Civilized human beings, said Leopold Tyrmand, should "agree not to burden each other" with their "excessive humanity."

Viewing U.S. foreign policy as an instrument for reform rather than of stability is not only arrogant; it also ignores the severely limited capacity of any external agency to influence and reshape alien cultures. As Gunnar Myrdal pointed out in *Asian Drama: An Inquiry into the Poverty of Nations* (1968), the economic and political development of low-income countries is determined largely by internal forces—static and dynamic—though well-considered trade, investment, and aid from industrial states may spur development. Any government has the right to request American or Russian technical assistance. By the same token, Washington and Moscow have the right to accept or turn down the request. The provision of economic or military aid that serves the interests of both parties presents few problems. It is wrong, however, for the donor government to give, withhold, or modify aid to force significant domestic changes unacceptable to the recipient regime and unrelated to the efficient use of the assistance.

The crusading impulse to reform should be clearly distinguished from the humanitarian motive that has prompted the U.S. government over the years to do more for the foreign victims of famine, earthquake, and war than any other in history. Earthquake relief is not designed to restructure institutions, overthrow regimes or promote "free elections."

* * *

Soft moralism tends to associate virtue with weakness, just as it associates vice with power. Western morality affirms the fundamental worth of the poor and the weak and recognizes that they are less able to defend their rights than the rich and powerful. Further, under the rubric of noblesse oblige men privileged by wealth or station are duty-bound to protect and assist the lowly. But this does not automatically endow the weak with innocence or virtue, whether they are deprived by nature, sloth, exploitation, or other circumstances.

The behavior of all states—great and small—must be judged by the same moral yardstick, recognizing that the degree of responsibility is commensurate with the capacity to act. "He who has much given to him will have much required of him." Yet, there is a widespread tendency among moralistic Americans to regard the fledgling new states with a kind of perverse paternalism which excuses childish, demanding, and otherwise irresponsible behavior, such as that of the delegates who applauded the expulsion of Taiwan from the United Nations in 1971 or those who charged Washington and Brussels with "deliberate genocide" and "massive cannibalism" for rescuing more than 2,000 innocent foreign hostages of nineteen nationalities in the Congo in 1964.

Neither the weak nor the strong are immune from error or corruption. The celebrated and much confessed "arrogance of power" should not blind us to the arrogance of weakness, which may express itself in simple claims of virtue, insistence on unjustified "reparations," or demands for minority control, all calculated to exploit a pervasive sense of guilt in the American character. As Churchill pointed out, we Anglo-Saxons tend to feel guilty because we possess power. Prime Minister Nehru and other Third World spokesmen often assumed an air of moral superiority, insisting they were uncorrupted by power and therefore possessed an innocence and humanity denied the leaders of powerful, and hence guilty, states. In a U.N. speech in 1960, Premier Saeb Salaam of Lebanon said: "We, the small, uncommitted nations, can perhaps take a more objective view of the world situation. We can judge international issues with comparatively greater detachment and impartiality; in a sense, the small uncommitted nations can be said to represent the unbiased conscience of humanity." [2]

Recent official Swedish statements reflect this moralistic tendency. Though espousing neutrality, Swedish officials have been quick to condemn the behavior of the big powers, particularly the United States, and to take "moral" stands on a variety of international issues. Stockholm has supported Hanoi and the Vietcong against America and has given moral and material aid to the Communist-assisted guerrilla fighters seeking to overthrow Western-oriented regimes in southern Africa. In November 1971, the Swedish government decided to prohibit arms shipment to insurgent groups in Africa so as not to become directly involved and thus remain "neutral." It is morally easy for politicians or religious leaders to cheer and condemn from the sidelines when they have no responsibility and are unwilling to become committed. With studied hyperbole John P. Roche makes the point: "Power corrupts. And the absence of power corrupts absolutely."

* * *

[2] *New York Times,* October 5, 1960.

The prevailing moralistic approach tends to be preoccupied with the present, neglectful of the past, and nonchalant about the future. Impatient with imperfection, the new romantics indulge in what Elton Trueblood has called the "sin of contemporaneity." It may be argued that enchantment with the chronological now represents a positive contribution from the existential emphasis on the present-tense imperative, but evidence suggests it is usually an escape from the eternal now which binds the past and future in an endless chain of responsibility.

According to classical morality, man is not an isolated actor suddenly thrust onto an alien stage and expected to respond to the strange sights and sounds around him. Man is born and nurtured in an ongoing community, a continuous web of cause and effect, a tapestry of gifts and expectations. Man is a creature of history, a product of the past, an actor in the present, and an influence for the future. To reject the past, as so many radicals do, is to reject the fabric of human continuity that gives moral meaning to the present.

The widespread and strangely indiscriminate view that the status quo is bad and change is good suggests that history is "a tale told by an idiot," a story without meaning. Western morality insists that history, like man, is morally ambiguous and that the task of the present generation is to accept the best of the past and reject the worst. This selective dependence on history is not possible if there is no understanding of the major ideas, events, and forces that have shaped the present. Many students today show no interest in the developments that had the most dramatic impact on the political outlook of their parents. If events like Pearl Harbor, Korea, and the Budapest Uprising are not known or have no common meaning, how can the two generations communicate?

The understanding of recent history is vital, even if earlier eras must be short changed. This suggests the advisability of teaching history backward, starting with today's newspaper and covering the past decade before moving to the more distant past.

*   *   *

In their disdain for history, ancient and recent, and their insistence on achieving quick solutions, many romantic idealists sell the future short by neglecting the disciplines of moral and political calculation. The principal practical test of any political decision is not the intention of the actor or the means he uses, but the immediate and long-range consequences of his decision. These consequences are also essential in making a moral assessment of the decision.

Moral choice demands calculation—an assessment of multiple causes, multiple alternatives, and multiple consequences. Seemingly good courses often have disastrous results. Many critics of U.S. defense policy condemned the announced underground nuclear test which was carried out in Alaska in November 1971. Some said it would trigger a devastating earthquake or tidal wave or otherwise damage the natural environment. Other critics insisted that the test was a giant step in accelerating the strategic arms race. After careful calculation President Nixon decided to go ahead, convinced that the natural risks had been exaggerated and that the probable consequences were on balance good for U.S. security and world peace. After the test there was no indication of a radioactive leak, and the damage to the environment appeared to be slight. The test did demonstrate the feasibility of the Spartan warhead, an essential component in any viable ABM system designed to protect

America's land-based Minuteman missiles. These missiles in turn are designed to deter a nuclear attack against this country and thus avoid a conflagration. Further, the test may well have strengthened the U.S. position at the Strategic Arms Limitation Talks with the Russians, which are seeking to control offensive and defensive nuclear weapons on both sides. These and many other factors were considered in the calculus preceding the president's decision. Unlike the president, the critics do not bear the burden of decision, but are they not obligated to consider all the major issues at stake before they pronounce final moral judgments?

*   *   *

Some of the more extreme American moralists, baffled by complexity and impatient with the untidy state of the world, sometimes adopt what amounts to a devil-theory of politics, an ever-popular version of the single-issue approach. They attempt to identify the central flaw, the fatal error, the demonic force underlying our present plight.

The earlier rational idealists discovered a series of plausible devils that, separately or in combination, were held responsible for war, injustice, poverty, and many other afflictions of mankind. Each was fatally vulnerable to its rational and righteous counterpart. The prince of darkness, capitalism, could be slain by socialism. The confusion of tongues, the cause of international misunderstanding and conflict, could be cured by education and Esperanto. Nationalism could be exorcised by internationalism and world government. The military and the "merchants of death" could be abolished by the renunciation of war. The winding road from Versailles to Pearl Harbor and beyond is cluttered with the debris of well-intentioned crusades—the League of Nations, the Kellogg-Briand Pact, and compulsory arbitration of inter-state disputes, to name a few. The idealists and their ideal solutions failed. The Wilsonians, it has been said, reached for utopia and gave us hell.

The targets of present-day devil-theorists bear a striking resemblance to those of earlier decades. Now it is the military-industrial complex, the establishment, the system, the corporate structure, technology, or greed. For many of the radical dissenters, the chief demon is "decadent liberalism" a menacing Mephistopheles embracing all the vices of gradualism, reform, due process, and peaceful evolution—benign bourgeois beatitudes that blur the necessity to "destroy the system" and thus subvert revolutionary zeal. Some zealots prefer more personal devils, such as Lyndon Johnson, Dean Rusk, or Richard Nixon. By the same token, they have personal messiahs such as Mao, Ho, and Che.

The devil-theory approach lends itself to an apocalyptic interpretation of the political situation. The whole world is polarized and the golden mean, the vital center, and orderly change are thrown to the winds. The forces of good (read progressive or revolutionary) at home and abroad are arrayed against the forces of evil (read status quo or reactionary) and there is no compromise. The "establishment" will be crushed and "the people" will prevail. It is only a matter of time and dedication. Here one sees the rhetoric of the Maoists and Marxists being used loosely and without discipline by the soft romantics.

*   *   *

Most American moralists have an inadequate understanding of the limits and possibilities of logic, rationality, and calculation. According to classical Western

norms, moral reasoning is a possibility, indeed a necessity. Man is a reasoning creature. Within the limits of
circumstance, he can plan, devise, calculate, though he
can rarely control or determine events. Circumstances are
too complex and intractable and human emotions too
unpredictable to come up with solutions. Precise predic-
tion is impossible and risk is never absent. Tolstoy
dramatizes the human situation by describing the dilemma of a military commander who

> . . . is always in the midst of a series of shifting events and so he
> never can at any moment consider the whole import of an event
> that is occurring. Moment by moment the event is imperceptibly
> shaping itself, and at every moment of this continuous, uninter-
> rupted shaping of events the commander in chief is in the midst of
> a most complex play of intrigues, worries, contingencies, authori-
> ties, projects, counsels, threats, and deceptions and is continually
> obliged to reply to innumerable questions addressed to him, which
> constantly conflict with one another.[3]

To acknowledge the serious limits of rational calculation in politics is not to deprecate reason, or the necessity
to marshal relevant facts, or the desirability of projecting
the probable consequences of competing lines of action.
Politics is more an art than a science, but the scientific
discipline of weighing evidence is a compelling moral
obligation. To ignore evidence, to disdain logic, or to
overlook empirical data is to retreat into blind emotion
which spawns illusions. If the romantics fail to discipline
their desires with data or their passions with power and
persist in their illusions, they become almost indistin-
guishable from cynics or nihilistic trouble makers.

Just as the contemporary sentimentalists expect too
little of reason, the earlier rational idealists expected too
much. Reason provides the capacity to conceive of noble
ends and to comprehend the barriers to their fulfillment,

[3] Leo Tolstoy, *War and Peace* (New York: Simon and Schuster, 1942),
pp. 921-22.

19

but reason cannot provide the will or the capacity to behave responsibly. Reason is not an independent human agency that transcends the self, but rather a servant of the self with all its pride and prejudice. A morally sensitive statesman can enlist reason in the pursuit of wise and prudent policies. A morally corrupt politician can likewise enlist reason for his ignoble ends. The old utopians believed that reason and goodwill unaided by power would transform politics, but the new romantics seem to despair of reason altogether.

*   *   *

Western morality, in sum, affirms the dignity of man and the necessity for the state. It is precisely because man is finite and inclined to pursue his selfish desires at the expense of his neighbor that structures of order and justice are needed. The responsible state alone is capable of insuring that basic human rights will not be trampled underfoot.

The great majority of American people by temperament and their respect for law are committed to a domestic order rooted in a prudent balance of justice and freedom, and to an international order that is safe for diversity and peaceful change. Movement toward these political goals at home and abroad requires a working combination of the "impossible ideal" and an appreciation of political limitations. A man's aim should exceed his grasp, but not by too much. Our times call for idealism without illusion and realism without despair.

NATIONAL INTERESTS AND MORAL ABSOLUTES

Arthur Schlesinger, Jr.

For centuries theologians have distinguished between just and unjust wars, jurists have propounded rules for international conduct, and moralists have worried whether their own nation's course in foreign affairs was right or wrong. Yet the problem of the relationship between morality and international politics remains perennially unsettled. It is particularly difficult and disturbing for Americans today. The Vietnam war was first widely justified on moral grounds and is now widely condemned on moral grounds. Both judgments cannot be right. This contradiction and even more, of course, the horror of the war must surely compel us to look again at the moral question in its relation to foreign policy.

Williams James used to say that temperaments determined philosophies. People who respond to international politics divide temperamentally into two schools: those who see policies as wise or foolish, and those (evidently in the majority today) who see them as good or evil. One cannot claim an ultimate metaphysical difference here. No one can escape perceptions of good and evil, and no policy can achieve a total separation of political and moral principles. Nor in the impenetrability of one's heart can one easily know when political motives are moral motives in disguise or when moral motives are political motives in disguise. Still the choice of disguise reveals something about temperament and philosophy.

In this time when both right and left yield with relish to the craving for moral judgment, it may be useful to set forth a minority view. Should—as both supporters and critics of the Vietnam war have asserted—overt moral principles decide issues of foreign policy? Required to give a succinct answer, I am obliged to say: as little as possible. If in the management of foreign affairs, decisions can be made and questions disposed of on other grounds, so much the better. Moral values in international politics—or so, at least, my temperament enjoins me to believe—should be decisive only in questions of last resort. One must add that questions of last resort do exist.

*   *   *

How are right and wrong in dealings among sovereign states to be defined? Here the moralist of foreign affairs first has recourse to the moral code most familiar to him—the code that governs dealings among individuals. His contention is that states should be judged by principles of individual morality. As Woodrow Wilson put it in his address to Congress on the declaration of war in 1917, "We are at the beginning of an age in which it will be insisted that the same standards of conduct and of responsibility for wrong done shall be observed among nations and their governments that are observed among the individual citizens of civilized states." [1] John Foster Dulles said it even more bluntly, or naively, in the midst of World War II: "The broad principles that should govern our international conduct are not obscure. They grow out of the practice by the nations of the simple things Christ taught." [2]

The argument for the application of moral principles

[1] Address to Congress, April 3, 1917.
[2] John Foster Dulles, *A Righteous Faith for a Just and Durable Peace* (New York: Federal Council of Churches, 1942), p. 10.

to questions of foreign policy is thus that there is, or should be, an identity between the morality of individuals and the morality of states. The issues involved here are not easy. One cannot doubt, as I shall contend later, that there are cases in foreign affairs where moral judgment is possible and necessary. But one may also suggest that these are extreme cases and do not warrant the routine use of moral criteria in making foreign policy decisions. It was to expose such indiscriminate moralism that Reinhold Niebuhr wrote *Moral Man and Immoral Society* forty years ago. Though the lesson of this penetrating book appears to have been forgotten in this moralistic age, I cannot see that the passage of time has weakened the force of Niebuhr's analysis.

Niebuhr insisted that a distinction had to be drawn between the moral behavior of individuals and of social groups. The obligation of the individual was to obey the law of love and sacrifice; "from the viewpoint of the author of an action, unselfishness must remain the criterion of the highest morality." But nations cannot be sacrificial. Governments are not individuals. They are trustees for individuals. Niebuhr quotes Hugh Cecil's argument that unselfishness "is inappropriate to the action of a state. No one has a right to be unselfish with other people's interests." [3] Alexander Hamilton had made the same point in the early years of the American republic: "The rule of morality ... is not precisely the same between nations as between individuals. The duty of making its own welfare the guide of its actions, is much stronger upon the former than upon the latter. Existing millions, and for the most part future generations, are concerned in the present measures of a government; while the consequences of the private action

---

[3] Reinhold Niebuhr, *Moral Man and Immoral Society* (New York: Charles Scribner's Sons, 1932), pp. xi, 258, 267.

of an individual ordinarily terminate with himself, or are circumscribed with a narrow compass." [4]

In short the individual's duty of self-sacrifice and the state's duty of self-preservation are in conflict; and this makes it impossible to measure the action of states by a purely individualistic morality. "The Sermon on the Mount," said Churchill, "is the last word in Christian ethics. . . . Still, it is not on those terms that Ministers assume their responsibilities of guiding states." [5] This is not to say that might makes right. It is to say that the morality of states is inherently different from the morality of individuals. Saints can be pure, but statesmen must be responsible. As trustees for others, they must defend interests and compromise principles. In consequence politics is a field where practical and prudential judgment must have priority over simple moral verdicts.

*   *   *

Now it may be urged against this view that the tension between individual morality and political necessity has been, to a considerable degree, bridged within national societies. This takes place when the moral sense of a community finds embodiment in positive law. But the shift of the argument from morality to law only strengthens the case against the facile intrusion of moral judgment into foreign affairs.

A nation's law can set down relatively clear standards of right and wrong in individual behavior because it is the product of an imperfect but none the less authentic internal moral consensus. International life has no such broad or deep areas of moral consensus. It was once

---

[4] Alexander Hamilton, *Pacificus,* No. 4, July 10, 1793.

[5] Winston Churchill, *The Gathering Storm* (Boston: Houghton Mifflin Co., 1948), p. 320.

hoped that modern technology would create a common fund of moral ideas transcending the interests of particular nations—common concepts of interest, justice and comity—either because the revolution in communications would bring people together through fear of mutual destruction. Such expectations have been disappointed. Until nations come to adopt the same international morality, there can be no world law to regulate the behavior of states as there is law within nations to regulate the behavior of individuals. Nor can international institutions—the League of Nations or the United Nations—produce by slight of hand a moral consensus where none exists. World law must express world community; it cannot create it.

This is not to say we cannot discern the rudiments of an international consensus. Within limits, mankind has begun to develop standards for conduct among nations—defined, for example, in the Hague Conventions of 1899 and 1907, in the Geneva Protocol of 1925 and the Geneva Conventions of 1949, in the Charter and Covenants of the United Nations, in the Charter, Judgment, and Principles of the Nuremberg Tribunal, and so on. Such documents outlaw actions that the world has placed beyond the limits of permissible behavior. Within this restricted area a code emerges that makes moral judgment in international affairs possible up to a point. And within its scope this rudimentary code deserves, and must have, the most unflinching and rigorous enforcement.

But these international rules deal with the limits rather than with the substance of policy. They seek to prevent abnormalities and excesses in the behavior of states, but they do not offer grounds for moral judgment and sanction on normal international transactions (including, it must be sorrowfully said, war itself, so long as war does not constitute aggression and so long as the rules of warfare are faithfully observed). They may eventually promote a world moral consensus. But, for the present, national, ideological, ethical, and religious divisions remain as bitterly intractable as ever.

It must finally be observed that few problems in international politics are even cast in the mold for unequivocal ethical approval or disapproval. Most foreign policy decisions are self-evidently matters of prudence and maneuver, not of good and evil. "I do not think we can conclude," George Kennan noted a decade ago, "that it matters greatly to God whether the free trade area or the Common Market prevails in Europe, whether the British fish or do not fish in Icelandic territorial waters, or even whether Indians or Pakistanis run Kashmir. It might matter, but it is hard for us, with our limited vision, to know." [6] The raw material of foreign affairs is, most of the time, morally neutral or ambiguous. In consequence, for the great majority of foreign policy transactions, moral principles cannot be decisive.

If I may summarize the argument up to this point, I am constrained to doubt the easy applicability of personal moral criteria to most decisions in foreign policy, first, because governments in their nature must make decisions on different principles from those of personal morality; second, because no international moral consensus of sufficient depth and strength exists to sustain a comprehensive and binding international morality; and, third, because most issues of foreign affairs do not lend themselves to categorical moral verdicts.

* * *

But this is not all. It is not only that moral principles are of limited use in the conduct of foreign affairs. It is

[6] George F. Kennan, "Foreign Policy and Christian Conscience," *Atlantic*, May, 1959.

Jaspers, Karl. *The Future of Mankind*. Translated by E. B. Ashton. Chicago: University of Chicago Press, 1961.

Kaplan, Abraham. *American Ethics and Public Policy*. New York: Oxford University Press, 1963.

Kennan, George F. *American Diplomacy: 1900-1950*. Chicago: University of Chicago Press, 1951.

————.*Realities of American Foreign Policy*. Princeton: Princeton University Press, 1954.

Kissinger, Henry A. *The Necessity For Choice*. New York: Harper & Bros., 1960.

Koestler, Arthur. *Darkness at Noon*. New York: Penguin Signet Books, 1948.

Kristol, Irving. *On the Democratic Idea in America*. New York: Harper & Row, 1972.

Lefever, Ernest W. *Ethics and United States Foreign Policy*. New York: World Publishing Company, 1957.

Levine, Robert A. *The Arms Debate*. Cambridge, Mass.: Harvard University Press, 1963.

Little, David. *American Foreign Policy and Moral Rhetoric*. New York: Council on Religion and International Affairs, 1969.

Lippmann, Walter. *The Communist World and Ours*. New York: Little, Brown & Co., 1959.

Maritain, Jacques. *Man and the State*. Chicago: University of Chicago Press, 1951.

Marshall, Charles Burton. *The Exercise of Sovereignty*. Baltimore: The Johns Hopkins Press, 1965.

————.*The Limits of Foreign Policy*. Enlarged ed. Baltimore, The Johns Hopkins Press, 1968.

Miller, William Lee. *Piety along the Potomac*. Boston: Houghton Mifflin Co., 1964.

Morgenthau, Hans J. *Scientific Man vs. Power Politics*. Chicago: University of Chicago Press, 1946.

Morgenthau, Hans J., and Kenneth W. Thompson (eds.). *Principles and Problems of International Politics.* New York: Alfred A. Knopf, 1950.

Murray, John Courtney. *Morality and Modern War.* New York: Council on Religion and International Affairs, 1959.

Muste, A. J. *Not by Might.* New York: Harper & Bros., 1947.

Niebuhr, Reinhold. *The Children of Light and the Children of Darkness.* New York: Charles Scribner's Sons, 1944.

————. *The Irony of American History.* New York: Charles Scribner's Sons, 1952.

————. *Moral Man and Immoral Society.* New York: Charles Scribner's Sons, 1932.

————. *The Structure of Nations and Empires.* New York: Charles Scribner's Sons, 1959.

Nitze, Paul H., and Kenneth W. Thompson. *U. S. Foreign Policy: Ideals and Realities.* New York: Foreign Policy Association, 1959.

O'Brien, William V. *War and/or Survival.* Garden City, N.Y.: Doubleday and Co., Inc., 1969.

Osgood, Robert E. *Ideals and Self-Interest in American Foreign Relations.* Chicago: University of Chicago Press, 1953.

Osgood, Robert E., and Robert W. Tucker. *Force, Order, and Justice.* Baltimore: The Johns Hopkins Press, 1967.

Ramsey, Paul. *The Just War: Force and Political Responsibility.* New York: Charles Scribner's Sons, 1968.

————. *Who Speaks for the Church?* New York: Abingdon Press, 1967.

Thompson, Kenneth W. *Political Realism and the Crisis of World Politics.* Princeton: Princeton Univeristy Press, 1960.

Tillich, Paul J. *Love, Power and Justice*. New York: Oxford University Press, 1954.

Tocqueville, Alexis de. *Democracy in America*. 2 vols. New York: Alfred A. Knopf, 1945.

Tucker, Robert W. *The Just War: A Study in Contemporary American Doctrine*. Baltimore: The Johns Hopkins Press, 1960

Voeglin, Eric. *Science, Politics, and Gnosticism*. Chicago: Henry Regnery, 1968.

West, Charles C. *Ethics, Violence, and Revolution*. New York: Council on Religion and International Affairs, 1969.

Wolfers, Arnold. *The Anglo-American Tradition in Foreign Affairs*. New Haven: Yale University Press, 1956.

————. *Discord and Collaboration: Essays on International Politics*. Baltimore: The Johns Hopkins Press, 1962.

Library of Congress Cataloging in Publication Data
Main entry under title:

Ethics and world politics.

   (Christian A. Herter lecture series, 1971)
   (Washington Center of Foreign Policy Research.
   Studies in international affairs, no. 18)
   Bibliography: p.
   1. International relations—Moral and religious aspects—
   Addresses, essays, lectures.
   2. Vietnamese Conflict, 1961-   —United States—
   Addresses, essays, lectures.
   I. Lefever, Ernest W., ed. II. Series. III. Series:
   Washington Center of Foreign Policy Research.
   Studies in international affairs, no. 18.

JX1255.E75   172'.4   75–186511
ISBN 0-8018-1395-6
ISBN 0-8010-1400-6 (pbk.)

also that the compulsion to see foreign policy in moral terms may have, with the noblest of intentions, the most ghastly of consequences. The moralization of foreign affairs encourages, for example, a misunderstanding of the nature of foreign policy. Moralists tend to prefer symbolic to substantive politics. They tend to see foreign policy as a means, not of influencing events, but of registering virtuous attitudes. One has only to recall the attempt, made variously by right and by left, to make recognition policy an instrument of ethical approval or disapproval.

This is only the lesser problem created by the moralization of foreign policy. The deeper trouble is inherent in the very process of pronouncing moral judgment. For the man who converts conflicts of interest and circumstance into conflicts of good and evil necessarily invests himself with moral superiority. Those who see foreign affairs as made up of questions of right and wrong begin by supposing they know better than other people what is right for them. The more passionately they believe they are right, the more likely they are to reject expediency and accommodation and seek the final victory of their principles. Little has been more pernicious in international politics than excessive righteousness.

Moral absolutism may strike at any point along the political spectrum. From the standpoint of those who mistrust self-serving ethical stances, John Foster Dulles and, say, Noam Chomsky are equal victims of the same malady. Both regard foreign policy as a branch of ethics. They end up as mirror images of each other. In the process of moral self-aggrandizement each loses the humility which is the heart of human restraint. Sir Herbert Butterfield, after observing that "moral indignation corrupts the agent who possesses it and is not calculated to reform the man who is the object of it," makes the essential point: "The passing of what purports to be a moral judgment—particularly a judgment which amounts to the assertion that they are worse men than I am—is not merely irrelevant, but actually immoral and harmful." It is "really a demand for an illegitimate form of power. The attachment to it is based on its efficacy as a tactical weapon, its ability to rouse irrational fervour and extraordinary malevolence against some enemy." [7]

Moralism in foreign policy concludes in fanaticism; and the fanatic, as Mr. Dooley put it, "does what he thinks th' Lord wud do if He only knew th' facts in th' case." It ends abroad with crusades and the extermination of the infidel. At home it perceives mistakes in political judgment as evidence of moral obliquity; the issue becomes not self-delusion or stupidity but criminality and treachery; it ends in ferreting out the reprobate as traitors or war criminals. Those whose views on foreign policy arise from convictions of their own superior righteousness should recall the warning of Chekhov's: "You will not become a saint through other people's sins."

*   *   *

If moral principles have only limited application to decisions of foreign policy, and if moral absolutism becomes a source of intolerance and fanaticism, then we are forced to the conclusion that decisions in foreign affairs must generally be taken on other than moralistic grounds. It is necessary now to consider what these other grounds are. It will surprise no one familiar with this controversy in other years if one declares the belief that, where the embryonic international community cannot

[7] Herbert Butterfield, *History and Human Relations* (London: The Macmillan Co., 1951), pp. 109-110.

regulate dealings among nations, the safest basis for decision in foreign policy lies not in attempts to determine what is right or wrong but in attempts to determine the national interest.

Though the idea is an old and honorable one, "national interest," despite the valiant efforts through the years of Walter Lippmann, George Kennan, and Hans Morgenthau, has become an alarming phrase in America in the 1970s. Mention it before students, and the audience shudders. The words should alarm no one. A moment's thought will show that every nation *must* respond to some sense of its national interest. No nation that rejects national interest as the mainspring of its policy can survive; nor, indeed, can any nation be relied upon that acts against its national interest. Without the magnetic compass of national interest there would be no regularity and predictability in international affairs. George Washington called it "a maxim founded on the universal experience of mankind, that no nation is to be trusted farther than it is bound by its interest." [8]

This is not to say that "national interest" is a self-executing formula providing an automatic answer to every perplexity of foreign affairs. Men can argue endlessly about the content of national interest. One man's national interest may be another man's poison. Still the idea is not totally open-ended. Every nation, for example, has a set of fairly definite strategic interests. One has only to reflect on the continuities of Russian foreign policy, whether directed by czars or commissars. When one moves to politics and economics, identification of national interest certainly becomes more debatable. Yet even here one notices that nations often preserve,

[8] George Washington to Henry Lawrens, Novermber 14, 1778, in J. C. Fitzpatrick (ed.), *Writings* (Washington, D.C.: Government Printing Office, 1936), pp. xiii, 256.

through changes of government and ideology, an impressive amount of continuity. In any case, the idea of national interest provides the focus and framework within which the debate can take place. It is the debate itself that gives the idea its content and, in a democracy, its legitimacy.

Obviously a government can take a greedy as well as an enlightened view of its nation's interest. Greed tends to become the dominant motive when there is disparity of power between nations: thus the history of imperialism. But there is a self-limiting factor in the concept of national interest. It cannot, unless transformed by an injection of moral righteousness, product ideological crusades for unlimited objectives. Any consistent defender of the idea of national interest must concede that other nations have legitimate interests too, and this sets bounds on international conflict. "You can compromise interests," Hans Morgenthau has reminded us, "but you cannot compromise principles." [9]

This self-limiting factor does not rest only on the perception of other nations' interests. It is reinforced by self-correcting tendencies in the power equilibrium which, at least when the disparity of power is not too great, prevent national interest from billowing up into unbridled national egoism. History has shown how often the overweening behavior of an aggressive state leads to counteraction on the part of other states determined to restore a balance of power. This means that uncontrolled national egoism generally turns out to be contrary to long-term national interest. Can it be persuasively held, for example, that Hitler's foreign policy was in the national interest of Germany? The imperialist states of nineteenth-century Europe have generally been forced to

[9] Hans Morgenthau, "The Primacy of the National Interest," *American Scholar*, Spring, 1949.

revise their notions as to where national interest truly lies. In time this may even happen to the Soviet Union and the United States.

For these reasons, it may be suggested that national interest, realistically construed, will promote enlightened rather than greedy policy. So a realist like Hamilton said that his aim was not "to recommend a policy absolutely selfish or interested in nations; but to show, that a policy regulated by their own interest, *as far as justice and good faith permit,* is, and ought to be, their prevailing one." [10] So a realist like Theodore Roosevelt could say, "It is neither wise nor right for a nation to disregard its own needs, and it is foolish—and may be wicked—to think that other nations will disregard theirs. But is wicked for a nation only to regard its own interest, and foolish to believe that such is the sole motive that actuates any other nation. It should be our steady aim to raise the ethical standard of national action just as we strive to raise the ethical standard of individual action." [11]

*   *   *

Both Hamilton and Roosevelt thus tempered their conception of national interest with moral considerations. They did so because, as realists, they knew that national self-assertion at the expense of the value and interests of others could lead to national disaster. They did so too no doubt because there is something emotionally frustrating about calculations of national interest as the basis for decision. As moral men, we prefer to feel that our actions spring from profound ethical imperatives. The Anglo-American tradition, in particular, has long been addicted to the presentation of egoism in the

[10] Hamilton, *Pacificus,* No. 4 (emphasis added).
[11] Theodore Roosevelt, Sixth Annual Message, December 3, 1906.

guise of altruism. And there is more to it than that. If one has an honest sense of moral concern or moral outrage, it seems idle—indeed, false—to deny this when supporting or censuring a foreign policy. For better or worse, moreover, democratic opinion rebels at the idea of the domination of policy by self-interest. "Let the people get it into their heads that a policy is selfish and they will not follow it," A. J. P. Taylor has wisely written. ". . . A democratic foreign policy has got to be idealistic; or at the very least it has to be justified in terms of great general principles." [1 2]

Nor is this cynicism. It may well be that the instinct among nearly all nations to refer their actions to abstract moral principles is an involuntary tribute to the existence of a world public opinion, a latent international consensus, that we must all hope will one day be crystallized in law and institutions. This is what Jefferson had in mind when the Declaration of Independence enjoined "a decent respect to the opinions of mankind." It is the point made in a prescient passage in the sixty-third *Federalist:*

An attention to the judgment of other nations is important to every government for two reasons: the one is, that, independently of the merits of any particular plan or measure, it is desirable, on various accounts, that it should appear to other nations as the offspring of a wise and honorable policy; the second is, that in doubtful cases, particularly where the national councils may be warped by some strong passion or momentary interest, the presumed or known opinion of the impartial world may be the best guide that can be followed. What has not America lost by her want of character with foreign nations; and how many errors and follies would she not have avoided, if the justice and propriety of her measures had, in every instance, been previously tried by the light in which they would probably appear to the unbiased part of mankind?

[1 2] A. J. P. Taylor, *Europe: Grandeur and Decline* (London: Harmondsworth, Penguin in association with H. Hamilton, 1967), p. 357.

For all these reasons, there is an irrepressible propensity to moral judgment in the field of foreign affairs. Nor, despite the perils of moral absolutism, is the moral critique of policy without value. It may provide an indispensable reminder that all policies are imperfect and all statesmen capable of self-deception. Indeed, the truly Christian perspective offers the best antidote to the moralistic fallacy of transforming expedients into absolutes. John C. Bennett tells us of the meeting of a delegation from the World Council of Churches with President Kennedy in 1962. The delegation brought a message to heads of states from the New Delhi Assembly of the Council; a paragraph called for the cessation of nuclear tests. When Kennedy read this passage, he responded by discussing his own dilemma: What should the United States do to assure its own security in view of the resumption of tests by the Soviet Union? Impressed, a member of the delegation said, "Mr. President, if you do resume tests, how can we help you?" Kennedy turned to him and said, "Perhaps you shouldn't." [13] Not all statesmen thus recognize the value of separating ultimate from immediate considerations and of preserving ideals in a world of distasteful compromise; but, if more did, the world would be spared much trouble.

*　　*　　*

In addition, there are certain problems in foreign policy, often the most important problems, with so clear-cut a moral character that moral judgment must control political judgment—questions of war crimes and atrocities, of the nuclear arms race, of colonialism, of racial justice, of world poverty. Some of these problems

[13] John C. Bennett, *Foreign Policy in Christian Perspective* (New York: Charles Scribner's Sons, 1966), p. 12.

have already been defined in international documents. Others define themselves when the consequences of decision transcend the interests of individual nations and threaten the very future of humanity. Modern weapons technology has notably enlarged the number of problems demanding the moral priority: for the nuclear bomb, the ICBM, and MIRV, by virtue of their unimaginable powers of indiscriminate destruction, have gone far beyond the limits of prudential decision. Still other essentially moral problems arise—though perhaps I may find less agreement here—when civilized values of tolerance and human dignity are menaced by powerful armed fanaticisms whose victory would abolish intellectual and civil freedom in great areas of the world. I have in mind such movements as Nazism and Stalinism.

These moral considerations should control the idea of national interest; but they should not supersede it. Dr. Bennett in his wise and modest book *Foreign Policy in Christian Perspective* has made the proper distinction: "We may say that Christian faith and ethics offer ultimate perspectives, broad criteria, motives, inspirations, sensitivities, warning, moral limits rather than directives for policies and decisions." [14] I cannot think of any recent problem in our foreign policy that could not have been adequately and intelligently disposed of on the grounds of national interest, qualified as Hamilton and Roosevelt would have us qualify it. We are asked to consider such questions as when a nation is justified in using force beyond its frontiers or in providing armed support of or opposition to revolutions in other countries. Plainly such questions cannot be answered by a priori moral principles but only by careful case-by-case assessment. Burke long ago pointed out the difference between the statesman and the moralist: "The latter has

[14] *Ibid.*, p. 36.

only a general view of society; the former, the statesman, has a number of circumstances to combine with those general ideas, and to take into his consideration. Circumstances are infinite, are infinitely combined, are variable and transient. ... A statesman, never losing sight of principles, is to be guided by circumstances." [15]

It is through the idea of national interest that moral values enter most effectively into the formation of foreign policy. Here the function of morality is to clarify and civilize conceptions of national interest. Morality primarily inheres, in short, in the content a nation puts into its idea of national interest.

The moral question arises particularly in a state's observance or nonobservance of its own best standards. Foreign policy is only the face a nation wears to the world. If a course in foreign affairs implies moral values incompatible with the ideals of the national community, either the nation will refuse after a time to sustain the policy, or else it must abandon its ideals. A people is in bad trouble when it tries to keep two sets of books— when it holds one scale of values for its internal polity and applies another to its conduct of foreign affairs. The consequent moral schizophrenia is bound to convulse the homeland. This is what happened to France during the Algerian War. It is what is happening to the United States because of the Vietnam war.

*   *   *

This is a long way round to the Vietnam war; but it may offer a way into some of the perplexities raised by this horrid conflict. It should be evident, for example, that in order to condemn this war it is not necessary to

[15] Quoted in Colin Bingham (ed.), *Men and Affairs* (Sidney: Currawong, 1967), p. 69.

deliver a moral judgment on it. If our policy had been founded on a sober and deliberate calculation of the national interest, we could hardly have sunk so deeply and unthinkingly into a situation where our commitment so far exceeds any rational involvement of that interest or any demonstrable threat to our national security. This is why the analysts who have most consistently invoked the idea of the national interest—Lippmann, Kennan, and Morgenthau—have been skeptical about the Indo-Chinese adventure from the start.

I do not suggest that the advocates of the adventure did not have a national-interest argument too. That argument in its most sophisticated version was that, with the establishment of nuclear balance between America and Russia, the main source of world instability lay in Third World wars—the kind that Khrushchev called "national liberation" wars in the truculent speech of January 1961 which had so unfortunate an effect on the Kennedy Administration—and that, if the United States proved its ability to deal with such wars, then the world could look forward to an age of peace. The trouble with this argument was that it assumed Communist activity everywhere to be at the behest of and for the benefit of the Soviet Union. It gravely underestimated the strength of national communism, and it wildly overestimated the capacity of the United States to win guerrilla wars.

The further trouble was that, as the argument was put in political form, it was translated into an exceedingly crude series of propositions. Our national interest was involved, we were given to understand, because the Vietcong and Hanoi were the spearheads of a planned system of Chinese expansion. Therefore, by fighting in Vietnam, we were holding the line against an aggressive Red China. If we did not fight, we would, like Chamberlain at Munich, invite further aggression; and a billion

Chinese armed with nuclear weapons (a specter invoked with relish by Secretary Rusk) would overrun Asia and turn the world balance of power permanently in favor of communism. "The threat to world peace," as Vice-President Humphrey summed up this fantasy as late as October 1967, "is militant, aggressive Asian communism, with its headquarters in Peking, China. . . . The aggression of North Vietnam is but the most current and immediate action of militant Asian communism." [16]

The argument that Asian communism was a monolithic movement run out of Peking was preposterous at the time. It is more preposterous in these days of ping-pong diplomacy. As even William Buckley has managed to discern, President Nixon's China policy abolishes the major strategic argument for the Vietnam war.

Since it is painful to charge our national leaders with stupidity, one must suppose that this foolish analysis of the relation of Indo-China to the American national interest was only a secondary motive for our involvement in Indo-China. The primary motive, it seems probable in retrospect, had little to do with national interest at all. It was rather a precise consequence of the belief that moral principles should govern decisions of foreign policy. It was the insistence on seeing the civil war in Vietnam as above all a moral issue that led us to construe political questions in ethical terms, local questions in global terms, and relative questions in absolute terms.

The propensity toward thinking big in foreign policy was implicit in the Wilsonian tradition. The habit of ideological escalation grew in the early years of the Cold War. It became rampant in the era of the hymn-singing Presbyterian who served as secretary of state in the 1950s. The Kennedy Administration vacillated between

[16] *New York Times,* October 16, 1967.

the impassioned rhetoric of the inaugural address and Kennedy's own acute sense of the limitations of American power. Then Kennedy was murdered while he was still in the process of giving American foreign policy new precision and restraint. With his successors moralism became triumphant. I recognize that other pressures cooperated in the Indo-China catastrophe—above all, the momentum of the military machine, with its institutional conviction that political problems have military solutions, its institutional desire to try out weapons, tactics, and personnel, and its institutional capacity for self-delusion about the ability of just one more step of escalation to assure military success. Still the opportunity to shape policy seized with such avidity by the military was created by those who believed that America was in Vietnam on a moral mission—who applauded when President Johnson cried in 1965:

History and our own achievements have thrust upon us the principal responsibility for protection of freedom on earth. . . . No other people in no other time has had so great an opportunity to work and risk for the freedom of all mankind.[17]

The Vietnam war was a morality trip; and moral absolutism was the final stop. As early as 1965, the *New York Times* quoted an American pilot: "I do not like to hit a village. You know you are hitting women and children. But you've got to decide that your cause is noble and that the work has to be done."[18] In this anointed spirit we conceived ourselves the world's judge, jury, and executioner and did our work in Indo-China.

*   *   *

[17] Lyndon B. Johnson, *Public Papers of the President* (Washington, D.C.: Government Printing Office, 1966), vol. I (1965), p. 180.
[18] *New York Times,* July 7, 1965.

The moralistic cant of Presidents Johnson and Nixon helped delude a lot of pilots into supposing they were doing God's work. This experience should suggest the perils of moral absolutism in foreign affairs. Unfortunately, instead of strengthening the national-interest wing of the opposition to the war, Vietnam seems to have incited an equally moralistic outburst on the part of the war's most clamorous critics. Too many people on both sides of the Indo-China debate feel they know exactly what the Lord would do if He only knew the facts in the case.

Yet may not these critics, emotional and extravagant as they often are, have a point? If it is not necessary to make moral judgments in order to condemn the Vietnam war, may it not be necessary on other grounds? Are not even those quite satisfied to oppose the war as contrary to our national interest still obliged to face the question whether it may not be an immoral as well as a stupid war? I think they are. I think the nation must face the question if we are ever to extract the full and awful lesson from this catastrophe.

My own answer to the question is yes, it is an immoral war, and it became so, ironically, when our moralistic zeal burst the limitations the idea of national interest might have imposed on the conduct of the war. Our original presence in South Vietnam hardly seems immoral, since we were there at the request of the South Vietnam government. Nor does it seem necessarily contrary to our national interest; conceivably it might have been worth it to commit, say, 20,000 military advisers if this could preserve an independent South Vietnam. But at some point the number of troops, and the things they were instructed to do, began to go beyond the requirements of national interest. This point was almost certainly the decision taken in early 1965 to send our bombers to North Vietnam and our combat units to South Vietnam and thus to Americanize the war.

Theologians talk about the principle of proportionality—the principle that means must have a due and rational relationship to ends. The Vietnam war became, in my view, what can properly be called an immoral war when the means employed and the destruction wrought grew out of any conceivable proportion to the interests involved and the ends sought. Enjoined by our leaders as to the sublimity of the mission, we cast ourselves as saviors of human freedom, misconceived the extremely restricted character of our national stake in Indo-China, and, step by step, intensified senseless terror, until we stand today as a nation disgraced before the world and before our own posterity.

How will our descendants ever understand the mood in which ordinary GIs, inflamed with the belief that anything Americans did was right, virtuously massacred Indo-Chinese women and children—and in which such crimes were acquiesced in, if not concealed by, the theater command? How will they understand the mood in which some American citizens hailed a hysterical killer as a national hero and proposed that, instead of conviction by a military court-martial, he should have received the Congressional Medal of Honor? How will historians explain national decisions, piously taken by God-fearing men in air-conditioned offices in Washington, that resulted in the detonation over this weak and hapless land of 6 million tons of explosives—three times as much as we dropped on Germany, Italy, and Japan during World War II?

For years we averted our eyes from what we were doing in Indo-China—from the search-and-destroy missions and the free-fire zones, from the defoliation and the B-52s, from the noncombatants slaughtered, the villages laid waste, the crops and forests destroyed, the refugees, one third of the population of South Vietnam, huddled in unimaginable squalor, from the free and continuous violations of the laws of war. For years we even refrained from pursuing the question why we were fighting in Indo-China—the question that will mystify future historians as they try to figure out what threat to national security, what involvement of national interest, conceivably justified in the eyes of two presidents the longest war in American history, the systematic deception by American leaders both of themselves and of the American people, the death of thousands of Americans and hundreds of thousands of Vietnamese.

The Calley trial at last compelled the nation to begin to accept these questions. The days of pretending were over. No one can doubt that the ordeal of self-interrogation, however damaging it may be to our self-image and self-illusions, will be profoundly beneficial to our nation. If we have the fortitude to carry this process through, history may conclude that the brave men who died in Vietnam did not altogether die in vain.

*   *   *

Americans will have to come to terms with the unquestionable immorality of the Vietnam war. How we will do this is not at present clear. At the very least, a full inquiry into the causes and consequences of the war, as suggested by the *New Republic*,[19] would force the nation to contemplate seriously and intensely the things we have done in Indo-China and the things we must do to provide reparation for our acts and safeguards against their repetition.

[19] "Wanted: An Inquiry Into the War," *New Republic*, May 22, 1971.

But such an inquiry, one must trust, will not result in the vindication of the moral approach to foreign policy. One must hope rather that it would increase skepticism about moral judgments promiscuously introduced into international politics. One must hope that the Indo-China experience will inoculate the nation against the perversion of policy by moralism in the future.

Moral values do have a fundamental role in the conduct of foreign affairs. But, save in extreme cases, that role is surely not to provide abstract and universal principles for foreign policy decisions. It is rather to illuminate and control conceptions of national interest. The righteousness of those who apply personal moral criteria to the relativities and complexities of international politics can degenerate all too easily into absolutism and fanaticism. The assumption that other nations have traditions, interests, values, rights, and obligations of their own is the beginning of a true morality of states. The quest for values common to all states and the embodiment of these values in international covenants and institutions is the way to establish a moral basis for international politics.

This will not happen for a long, long time. The issues sundering our world are too deep for quick resolution. But an intelligent regard for one's own national interest joined to unremitting respect for the interests of others seems more likely than the invocation of moral absolutes to bring about greater restraint, justice, and peace among nations.

II. FORCE AND POLITICAL RESPONSIBILITY

Paul Ramsey

Men live, it seems, in different worlds. Intellectuals seek truth. Politicians seek power. Moralists pursue the right and the good. Artists create and savor beauty. Clergymen and churchmen proclaim the word of God and yearn to see an increase of true piety in the land. Each seeks not truth alone or power alone or beauty alone or piety alone, but these things with their inherent fruits and fitting consequences for the humanity of man.

Among these realms of human meaning and activity, everyone must make an ordering for himself and trace out the interconnections. There is no clear way for our society as a whole to determine the priorities to be assigned these values, not even by the clumsy yet decisive procedure of an annual struggle over the budget. Truth and goodness and piety are not exactly budget items. Hence, the question of how to speak truth or righteousness or piety to power is a question constantly in process of being asked and answered in inchoate and rather mysterious ways by a people as a whole and by each individual.

Yet each of these realms of activity and meaning are *res publica;* they are things that make a people. At the outset we ought not to fix gulfs and irremediable conflicts between them. We should not accept Hans Morgenthau's recent dictum that "truth threatens power, and power threatens truth." [1] Nor should we say that morality threatens power, and power threatens morality;

[1] Hans Morgenthau, *Truth and Power* (New York: Frederick A. Praeger, 1970).

or that statesmen have only the options of heeding, silencing, discrediting, or corrupting the true and the good. That assumes that truth and morality are external standards to be imposed on the political act as upon recalcitrant matter or an alien instrument.

Instead, there is political truth which intellectuals should attend to before rushing to judgment. And there may be modalities of morality in the use of power and in the art of government which moralists should discern that are specifically yet not generically different from the right and the good to be shown forth and accomplished in other sorts of human behavior.

We need to examine the nature of the political act, to anatomize the meaning and purpose of government. We need to ask if anything of importance can be said generally about the statesman, his vocation, and his duties; about the role and relations of a "politician" in the classical meaning of that word—one who serves and is an agent of the "polity." In old-fashioned language, who is a greater or lesser *magistrate?* What are his capacities and responsibilities? Under what sign or appointment or calling is to be placed the conduct of magisterial or political office? Are there any unchanging modalities of statescraft? How and what should our schools teach the potential leaders of the country? Indeed, the answer to the last question would be one part of the answer, if there is an answer, to the ancient questions: How is excellence in practical wisdom taught? How does one become just and virtuous and wise?

By now, you would suspect, if it had not already been said, that I am something of a religious thinker. I shall not set that aside now, nor try to speak as anything else. I can only say some few of the things that seem to me, as Christian theological ethicist, right to say about politics. I shall not take up any practical question without first disclosing the ultimate context in which, in my view, all such questions should be asked, if they are profitably to be addressed at all. I take comfort in the thought that I can make no more egregious error that that of a colleague of mine at Princeton, in the Department of Politics, who seems to believe that international law is Richard Falk's morality! [2] So are we moralists all, and, according to no less a theological authority than the U.S. Supreme Court, religious as well!

A statesman, however—to use Dean Acheson's elegant expression—is "present at the Creation." He is also present at the Fall. He is present at the Tower of Babel. He is present at the covenant God made with Noah, placing certain instruments of enforcement in his hands for the preservation of the world over which then the rainbow was set. In speaking of these stories, I may sound like a literalist. I claim rather to be a mythologist, who happens to believe that there is more light and truth concerning the political task of mankind to be found in these myths than in any number of theorems about politics consecutively arranged, or in any amount of "systems analysis" or decision-making with or without the assistance of computers. The same is doubtless true of other great cultural myths as well; but these are ours.

It is safe to say, I judge, that when the power of these stories is at the end of its tether, modern Western man will be at the end of his tether. There is "metaphysi-

---

[2] In a review of Telford Taylor's *Nuremberg and Vietnam* in the *New York Times Book Review,* December 27, 1970, Professor Richard Falk calls for "an *external* process of inquiry and judgment" into U.S. conduct of the war in Vietnam. Such an international Commission of Inquiry would represent an "authoritative" collective judgment of mankind as a whole. Yet this would not be a *tribunal;* it would not be punitive or a way of enforcing international law said to have been violated. The purpose instead would be "to expose, clarify, and repudiate" conduct. Thus, the "main objective of a war crimes approach" would be "to achieve a measure of rectitude as a result of *moral clarification*" (italics in original).

cal chaos" at the root of the present chaos of moral and political criteria. Today, at least everyone can claim like anyone to be an authority on good and evil; yet we are unable to agree on how we even *might* agree on moral and political questions. Where once we had agreed procedural values plus private, substantive moral and political values clashing in the public forum, now the procedural values as well have been placed under massive assault by the private opinions of what Madison called minority or majority "factions." There is thinly disguised, limitless war of all against all other "moral" men. Such chaos in our sense of political limits can finally be traced home to the decline in the power of these biblical stories in silently forming the imagination and shaping the sensibilities of Western man.

Instead of taking these stories to be either literally or mythically true, you are welcomed to regard them as legends and fantasies. I suggest only that you join me in the thought-experiment of asking what would be the contours of man's political task on the underside of these myths *if* they were true of the human condition. I ask you to think *as if* you with all men are to be present at political creation, at the Fall, at Babel, and with Noah after the evil propensities of men's hearts in that generation deservedly ended in the first destruction—and the end of that end was government. What then would government mean?

Anyway, I seriously suggest the following scenario to heighten our imaginations. You and a CIA man are the last two men alive, you having been a high-ranking ambassador, or a lesser light, a worker for economic development in the Third World, or a position-paper writer in the State Department. There the two of you are, after a vast nuclear holocaust, or roasting the last potato over the last dying embers of a universe run down according to the law of entropy. If you then wanted to understand in retrospect what had happened to your life and energies and hopes and the meaning of the political life of mankind, you could do nothing better than to read and ponder together Plato's *Republic* and the Bible.

Taken together, the myths of Genesis constitute, with increasing specificity as the story unfolds, one of the world's best commentaries on government, even as Madison said of government that it is an excellent commentary upon the human heart.

*   *   *

In their capacities as "magistrates" men exercise creative rulership. Political decision and action is in *the image of God,* who also rules by particular decrees. God does not create a world in general; he creates a specific world out of myriad possibilities that might have been. God says, "Let there be ..."; and there is some new shaping event put forth into the world. The political act calls the things that are to be into being from things that are not. In a very real sense, an exercise of statecraft is a creation *ex nihilo.* For all the doctrine and the policy research that went before, a statesman shapes events by decisions or indecisions that go beyond doctrine, that launch out into the unknown and the not-yet, and that do not pop out of research, game playing, or systems analysis. A statesman must actualize what is to be from among a number of legitimate choices, each of which is plausible before the event. He has the high and lonely responsibility of choosing what shall actually be done from among a number of possibilities, any of which might have been. To prove after the event that political decisions were right is rather like speculating what world history would have been if Cleopatra's nose had been longer, or like asking whether God should have created this world and not some other which any half-baked intellect can think of in a thrice.

This is only to say in religious terms what the Greeks said by distinguishing between two forms of practical wisdom. In one, practical reason is used to produce some artifact beyond the act itself—a poem, painting, sculpture, machine, or (as we say today) a product of "social engineering." That was called *making,* which has its rules. The other exercise of practical reason Aristotle called *doing.* Under this fall ethics and politics, and Aristotle wrote one unified ethico-political treatise to explain what he believed man's moral and political *conduct* was all about. Moral and political acts are important not for what they make or engineer beyond themselves—not for their routinized institutional remainders, so to speak—but for what they do in the world and because of the answering or negating responses these actions evoke in the community of mankind's conduct through time.

I conclude from this that government—the political act and the statesman's, the politician's, the magistrate's, the citizen's office—is a matter of the risk-filled venture of creatively doing something, not primarily making, engineering, manipulating, composing, or arranging anything at all. In this view, the political actor is not a mere maker of schemes that can be quantified, but rather a doer of deeds that brings out of nothing, beyond all rational calculation, the things he hopes to be. In this sense, it is humanly far better to have an enemy than a fellow technocrat. To be present at political creation is to be doers of the word—the word that calls into being events that are not—and not hearers only, not only hearers of exhaustive analysis of the alternatives.

Two lines in a parable of Jesus exhibit the difference between *making* and *doing,* and the difference between "counting the costs" in each case, although that was not the main point of the parable.

> For which of you desiring to build a tower, does not first sit down and count the cost, whether he has enough to complete it? Otherwise, when he has laid a foundation, and is not able to finish, all who see it begin to mock him saying, "This man began to build, and was not able to finish." (Luke 14: 28-30, RSV)

That reminds me of a discerning statement attributed to Dean Acheson when he retired from foreign policy formation, and among other things took up the more comfortable activity of furniture-making for relaxation. "A chair," he said, "is made to sit in: when you've made it you can tell whether you made it right; there is no such definitive test of the rightfulness of a political policy-decision." So Jesus spoke not of measurable calculation, or proof or disproof of one's ability to finish an edifice, when he mentioned the predicament of a king. Instead a king or statesman needs wise "counsel," not the sort of calculation that is sufficient for builders of towers or makers of chairs. He lives in a world of *doing*; he is going to encounter other *doings* that are always coming upon him and to which he must respond with some risk-filled, unmeasurable, creative decision which shapes the future in a way that cannot be definitely demonstrated to have been wise.

> Or what king, going to encounter another king in war, will not sit down first and take counsel whether he is able with ten thousand to meet him who comes against him with twenty thousand? And if not, while the other is yet a great way off, he sends an embassy and asks terms of peace. (Luke 14: 31-32, RSV)

The trouble is that in the world of encountering powers one *can* sometimes carry that off! Cromwell's decisive battle against Charles I was a case in point. In statecraft one sits down to take counsel, not to "count" or to make or to engineer the consequences. In politics there are no completed towers, no solutions, no finished edifices. There are only better or worse outcomes, some new eventuality put forth while going to meet the *doings,* the actions of other agents in the international system that are always coming upon us. A statesman must always, unlike builders of towers, posit his decision and action in a world in which there is always the action, interaction, and counteraction of others and other forces and influences coming upon him. These all, not he alone, determine the outcome; and then the outcome of one problem is again problematic in a network of continuing allied or encountering conducts. Foreign policy formation is a community of *doings,* creating new situations out of nothing; it is not a kind of *making* something out of altogether calculable pre-existent factors. Policy is not a conclusion to be drawn from the calculations of builders or *makers.* Statecraft is not primarily a matter of social engineering, of building institutions; it is rather a system of interacting *doings.* For this reason, ethics and politics belong together, while the dream of completely rationalized systems analysis would remove both.

It does not matter much whether we interpret political vocation in terms of the Biblical notion of creation beyond things that are or whether we interpret it in terms of Aristotelian practical wisdom pertaining to any sort of *doing.* Either provides a context of understanding in which one can ask, and hope a proper answer, the question: What is the relation of moral values to international politics? Our moral values are not inchoate things, soft items or factors to be composed into a package with other hard factors like national interests or security by engineers or *makers* of policy. Values are not among the facts in front of the eyes of the beholder or of the decision-maker, out there to be taken into account, accommodated, compromised, or yielded to by magistrates also responsible for the hard realities of the power and freedom of action of the nation-state. I can think of nothing worse than if there were a theologian- or moralist-in-residence in the Pentagon or State Department, or someone appointed to represent values in military or diplomatic game-playing, so that they be not forgotten. Then our values as a people would be things to be made into policy instead of moral purposes to be *done*. You can be sure what would be the result: moral values would be engineered out.

The next worse thing would be the present state of affairs, in which politicians or political scientists or nuclear scientists choose their favorite group of religious leaders or moralists; and theologians and moralists choose their favorite political leaders and scientists; and each group rushes headlong into *specific* policy debate, each contending that its particular reading of the fact-value situation is guaranteed by the True and the Good. This has led, I imagine, to more frequent use of the terms "moral" and "immoral" in U.S. foreign policy debate than ever before in the history of mankind, by amateurs who know little of the logic of moral reasoning and have thought little of the general principles and special modalities of political morality. This is not to suggest that everyone should be an expert in ethics, but only that this would have to be the case *if* (but only *if*) our moral values are "out there" as moments or factors that like the fact-situation can be calculated, each to be weighed against the other in composing or manufacturing political agency or government.

Instead, the truth is that moral considerations are behind the eyeballs of the statesman; they precede the exercise of calculating reason. The values of a people are within a statesman; they are not matter with which he deals or which he handles. The values of a people are the spirit and purposes animating the community, pervading its institutions and voluntary associations, forming consciences, including the consciences of citizen and magistrate alike. The values are in the ethos, the traditions of a people; they are inculcated by the institutions, the laws, the activities of the community; these are in charge of the upbringing of Socrates and any man who has lived in an Athens worth living in. Mr. C. S. Lewis in *The Abolition of Man* makes the striking statement: "I am very doubtful whether history shows us one example of a man who, having stepped outside traditional morality and attained power, has used that power benevolently." [3] That states the historic role of moral values in relation to politics better than any statement I know. Men get to know justice first of all through the *jus gentium* animating the historical community into which they are born; a man's conscience and moral sensibilities have their origin in identity with the purposes of a particular people. To step outside the morality that was handed down to us and then to attain power sets raw power against a weak and abstract morality and sets truth and goodness against power. Still, families, schools, churches, and the writers of a nation's songs should not mistake the most telling way in which anyone speaks truth and righteousness to decision-makers in power. That is through their upbringing and moral development in a society whose moral purposes, values, and outlook they (perhaps inarticulately) share.

*　　　*　　　*

But there is another question to be considered: Is there any necessary contradiction between Western ethical

---

[3] C. S. Lewis, *The Abolition of Man* (New York: The Macmillan Co., 1961), p. 78.

values and the pursuit of the national interest, including national security, within the interstate system? Since the division of mankind into cities, nation-states, and linguistic groupings came later than the creation, the answer to this question requires the introduction of themes in addition to the positive role of statecraft in bringing into being new forms of political action and interaction.

To be present at the Fall is to be present at Babel. Indeed, the story of the tower of Babel explicates the *political* consequences of the Fall. There was a time before time, so the story goes, when "the whole earth was of one language, and of one speech"—one people, no less. Here begins a little volume that might be entitled *The Necessity and the Frustrations of Power,* which should be placed in your libraries beside William Fulbright's *The Arrogance of Power,* Harland Cleveland's *The Obligations of Power,* and George Ball's *The Discipline of Power.* Men in that time long ago said, as say men in the eternal and recurring now: "Go to, let us build us a city, and a tower whose top may reach unto heaven; and let us make a name, lest we be scattered abroad upon the face of the whole earth." It is sad to report what happened to that first United Nations, at a time (if we are to believe the tale) far more auspicious than ours for the union of mankind and for the ability of peoples to understand one another. Instead, the Lord God (so the report reads) confounded their language, that they might not understand one another's speech—"and they left off to build the city" (Genesis 11:1-9).

The political life of mankind goes on perennially under the sign of the verdict at Babel. Politics in every age goes on as if that verdict has not been set aside. It is as if the study of international politics gives knowledge of the life of mankind on the underside of that divine decision. Every man calls to another, every group and nation responds to the other in the action-reaction syndrome, as they build in every age the City of Man. They strive for a vision of the whole, and agreement on this. Excellent plans and world-policies these are, some better than others. But it turns out that each thinks that he is making the plan for the center of the tower, for a City of Man that will include the rightful claims of all the rest, and he imagines his neighbor—the other actors in the interstate system—to be working on some peripheral part of the project. And vice versa, always vice versa! The vision each nation has is " a view of the universal"; none is "a universal view." So there is disagreement and dissention in the best of causes. Doubtless nothing men see of truth will ever be lost, but none will triumph as they wish. All have been subjected by the divine overruling which cunningly uses opposition to praise Him and to limit every nation's aspiration for omnipotence, or (as they say) security./The whole length and breadth of man's historical existence is lived on the underside of the verdict at Babel. A person with any religious discernment should also engage in every building operation in the earthly city with somewhat less expectation than the final unification of mankind. His political acts will be characterized by a sense of limitation; by an acceptance of the fact that we who build governmental organizations do not understand one another's speech or values nor do we look out upon even the common projects we have achieved with exactly the same eyes. God's No to man's attempt to build a tower-top reaching unto heaven was at the same time, I must conclude, a No to man's attempt (renewed by idealists in all ages) to reach world political unification. We do not live in the one world of the City of Man under construction.

This should free us for clear-sighted participation in politics for the meanwhile of man's historical existence.

Doubtless, statesmen are the workers on the foundation of some City of Man, but they will get along better if they do not presume to hope fully to understand one another. International congresses are babbling if the common interests and agreements of the represented nations are perilously poised over diverse particular concerns none of which will or should be given up entirely. Nothing in the nature of nuclear weapons, for example, has changed all this. The determination of history by the "means of destruction" is no more credible than the determination of history by the "means of production." Neither abolishes the role of nations or sets aside the divine overruling that said No to one earthly city.

Therefore I have one sharp, blunt answer to the question whether Western ethical values are compatible with the nation-state system and the pursuit of national interest and security within that system. If they are not compatible, those values have become unearthly and can in no way be politically effective. Doubtless the *existing* nation-state system can be improved, and structural arrangements can be introduced through which more inclusive human identification can pass. Still government suffers the rift and the blessing of the verdict at Babel. Doubtless there are values of universal spirit (art, religion, philosophy) that, as Hegel said, transcend the state; but to suppose that all our values do so and then to condemn the nation-state as an error is rather to condemn those values or our understanding of them by the touchstone of the truth of politics.

The assumption that government should aim at universal ideals is too much incorporated in that slogan of political realism which says that the task of statecraft is "the art of the possible." This suggests that if only enough of these possible accomplishments are laid end to end we will finally exit from the divisions which have been characteristic of the entire political life of mankind. It tempts our leaders, while responsibly performing the duties of their office, to announce that those offices and duties themselves are undergoing radical change; to announce that we are passing from "an era of confrontation" to "an era of negotiation,"—when the political truth is that confrontation is only another form of negotiation if ever there is anything vital enough to require negotiation, and when in fact we can expect only some new mix of these elements that are always going on in the international system.

Moreover, the tempered idealism in the realistic slogan that politics is the art of the possible is apt to become unleashed, to produce visionary prospects, and to render a people ungovernable when there is a time of waiting in the affairs of states, when outstanding problems seem not susceptible of solution, when the stresses and frustrations of power have to be patiently endured, and men seem not now to be destined to be present at some new political creation. Then even old men will dream dreams and claim these should be tried on the grounds that they are possible because the present realities are more harsh and unfruitful.

Remembering the fathers of the nations with whom we were present at Babel, we need to place beside the statement that politics is the art of the possible another statement that is equally true, namely, that politics is the art of the impossible. That also is what we are always attempting to do; so it was, is, and is to be in the collective actions of men: to make peace where there is no peace, to establish order to hold disorder at bay, to build the City of Man out of dissension and in the midst of fratricide (Augustine). Thus, a recent reviewer in the *New York Times* spoke of Great Britain's "outstanding success in non-successful diplomacy" and in attempting impossible tasks.[4] There are only a few nations, including our own, that have fallen heir to that responsibility on a worldwide scale—or heir to whatever portion of the "art of the impossible" needing to be done which we judge should be done *by us.*

Naturally, I prefer theological, mythical language to exhibit these realities. That is why I introduced the story about our fathers who were present at the primordial cleavage in the political life of mankind. In the present age, men are "not only *empowered* to set up states"; they are "also *condemned* to do so";[5] and that, it can easily be seen, is a blessing. For this reason, I say that unless Western ethical values are compatible with political life within the interstate system, they are compatible with no world at all in which you or your children's children will ever live. Of course, nations and empires rise and fall, disappear and coalesce. Alliances are made and endure for longer or shorter times. There may be leagues and unions of nations based solidly on the nation-state system (i.e., upon the confusion of tongues). There may be "parliaments of mankind" that are interstate arrangements but none of which are parliaments with universal legislative and enforcing power.

Still, the hope of setting up a world-state is an impermissible fanaticism. So also the idea, lately too often expressed by intellectuals, churchmen, newspaper editorials, and other leaders of opinion, that nations can simply break out of the "action-reaction syndrome" and prepare to respond instead to the intentions; indeed to the rectitude, of other nations and not to their possible

---

[4] Miles Copeland's review of Sir Humphrey Trevelyan's *The Middle East in Revolution,* in *New York Times Book Review,* January 31, 1971, p. 3.

[5] Helmut Thielicke, *Theological Ethics,* vol. II: *Politics* (Philadelphia: Fortress Press, 1969), p. 441.

actions and real capabilities. Armament for the security of the state, as well as *dis*armament for the security of the state, are subject to "the same law of move and countermove";[6] the same holds for interacting nuclear weapons as for interacting conventional weapons, and for the interrelation of offensive or defensive systems as well. Concerning the requirement that action always responds to action possibly coming upon us in the interstate system, there can be wide disagreement over what should be done. About the requirement itself, there can be none. Statesmen are not only morally *permitted* to put forth actions in conformity with the law of move and countermove; in the discharge of their political offices in this age, they are *condemned* to do so. That, it can easily be seen, is a blessing, because only the law of action-reaction prevents power from achieving omnipotence.

Therefore, a biblical view of politics does not deny that the rift in the world affects the state too. The cleavage that has occurred between being present at creation and being present at Babel means that, while government is ordained to guard against chaos and to insure a tolerable human collective existence, governments themselves under the same sign must be horizontally limited by other governments. Without power there could be no justice preserved through time; but power must be restrained and limited by further power, and not only by the consciences of men.

We can readily understand that if the United States and Russia together decide to levitate vertically and grasp world hegemony, or if the United States, Russia, and mainland China suddenly found an end to the limit each places upon the other's aspiration to omnipotence (or, as we say, security), if together we came close to completing the political constructions we are always building to high

[6] *Ibid.*, p. 490.

heaven, that would ineluctably mean on the horizontal plane the gravest possible injustice to the other peoples of the world, no matter how wise and morally sensitive we deem ourselves to be. Therefore, world hegemony (which is the only way to conceive of a world-state for as far as we can see down the stretches of future history) is ordinarily excluded from visions of a parliament of mankind. This means that we simply *stipulate* that mankind's vertical ascent to world community and world government shall be accomplished by including everyone without injustice to any.

The myth of Babel unravels such expectations and discloses them to be the dreams they are. An immanent limit in the peoples' sense of justice is not enough to place upon political power. Without external limits in "other sovereignties and state egoisms," without the frustrations of interstate pluralism, without recurring historical lessons in self-restriction, writes the German Lutheran theologian Helmut Thielicke, any government of a world community (no matter what its origin or internal arrangements) would take "a vertical turn" toward "unbridled upward expansion," arrogance, and boundless tyranny.[7] This is prevented by the blessing in the verdict at Babel according to which government, for man's good always, is subjected to the same rift that cleaved innocent creation from guilty human striving.

"Institutional good works" in the international order cannot hope to change this, any more than individual good works can save the human soul. This has to be said, even if there is room for many an institutional good work within the international system stripped of that impious addition to them. Man may introduce many improvements in the relations between the cities they are building, but they cannot remove the foundations of the

[7] *Ibid.*, p. 436.

political world in the requirement that arbitrary and unlimited power can be limited only by further power. That is a reflection of man's Babylonian heart. It is also a reflection of the merciful governance of God in ordaining and preserving mankind in commonwealths that are historically possible.

*   *   *

To be present at Babel is, then, to be present at the time of Noah when, more closely still, government was instituted to see mankind through to the end-time; and over that was set the rainbow of God's covenant, patience, and good pleasure. The crux, the essential element of government—whatever other good and more positive purposes it may serve—is said to be this: "Whoever sheds man's blood, by man shall his blood be shed, for in the image of God made he man" (Genesis 9:6, RSV). That alone holds the waters back from ever again becoming a flood, in a world history in which, we can be sure, God does not mean ultimately to yield to man's propensity to destruction and self-destruction. The Flood was once an emergency remedy; government is a remedy for all time.

The covenant with Noah placed in man's hands the awful instrument of rightfully shedding the blood of any man who sheds man's blood. That legitimates government's use of evil to restrain greater evil, which evil would be limitless but for the constraints of government authority, punishment, enforcement, and countervailing interstate encounters. The symbol is a bloody one, yet it should not be limited to its literal meaning. It certainly legitimates the use of "the sword" in the kingdom on God's left hand, through government by which he preserves the world after Babel. Capital punishment, however, need not be supposed to be endorsed for all time, among peoples who may be sufficiently agreed upon the objects of their common interests (Augustine's definition of *res publica*) and who have attained a sufficient degree of civilization. Even so, a residual right of capital punishment may never disappear, however we praise the attainment of its abolition. The general point, however, is that government's enforcement powers are never interrupted, its monopoly of power, its political use of coercion—and possibly of violence. Of such things the operation of the state consists, *ad intra* as well as *ad extra.*

To understand the bloody symbol the Bible uses for the role of government in using evil to prevent greater evil, and to understand God's rainbow-signal that this holds the world back from universal destruction and affords the context in which man's political creation can still go forward, we must understand that any coercion, any restraints, any enforcement, any resistance imposed upon the human spirit or on a human will is to be located on a continuum on which the shedding of blood is simply an extreme in the use of evil to prevent greater evil. From this perspective, a local community's interest in the education of its youth is good, while the fact that this cannot be accomplished simply by an orchestration of various voluntary participants, the fact that coercion is required is a necessary evil. Struggle and strife is in this age a normal aspect of anything that is done—e.g., conflict within and between governmental districts, with outcomes that must finally be enforced to attain sufficient compliance of those who disagree. That is an evil even if the end is good. Both the good and the evil are of the *esse* of government at any level. The shedding of the blood of those who shed human blood gives government the legitimate authority to use evil to punish evil, to threaten evil to prevent greater evil.

If you still dislike the metaphor, forget it—by remembering that for a Christian outlook the necessity of using any constraint at all was an evil needing justification. The need to use even nonlethal force upon the wills of other men in the organization of effective collective action could find warrant only because mankind's common creative ventures have fallen into confusion of tongues. The mandate of government is to set a limit to the self-destructiveness that otherwise would break out—in local school districts, in church as well as state, and in the interstate system. So the only real justice in the world is an ordered justice. As the Cambridge historian Herbert Butterfield put the point: Take the animosity characteristic of the average church choir, prolong it and give it a history, extend that animosity and "confusion of tongues" spatially, and you have an adequate explanation of all the wars of human history! That was the cause for the institution of government, politics, statecraft, and the magistrate's and the citizen's office: to use evil to hold greater evil at bay, so that within that context good can still be achieved, a common weal be preserved, and politically creative action be put forth with hope of success somewhat enduring.

To deny that the state possesses among its instruments the legitimate power to kill, to allege that that is a barbarism which modern progress has dissolved or can dissolve, to propagate the idea that there is no distinction to be drawn among actions that deal in coercion and death in the hope of thereby basically altering the nature of government—these beliefs, so long as the covenant with Noah endures and the world is preserved against the propensity of men to mutual destruction and self-destruction, can only result in the adoption of naive, nonpolitical notions of the vocation of politics. Such ideas critical of political realities find themselves criticized by those realities and finally rendered impertinent.

*　　*　　*

This is not the time to elaborate the moral and political criteria for deciding between a justifiable and an unjustifiable use of force in the international system. These criteria—the just war theory—are a matter of public record in the age-long literature of statecraft, especially in Christian writings on the political use of violence.

We can, however, profitably ponder the case of Lt. William L. Calley for what it discloses concerning our contemporary political malaise. I cite his testimony in his own behalf with no intention of commenting on the person or rendering ultimate judgement upon his acts. The melancholy fact is that the features of his case worth remarking on are entirely general ones, of which everyone is in some degree guilty who has not stood against the main currents of American political opinion. The first feature worth noting is that Calley claimed all orders are lawful, and that he never heard of an unlawful order, or a soldier's responsibility in relation to this distinction. Let us not associate that view only with the school of thought proclaiming "my country right or wrong", "when in war anything goes." It is also—and equally—a product of the idealistic notion that all war is an immoral activity of states, or of the view that a particular war is *ab initio* completely immoral even if, strangely said, it had to be fought. How could a truly lawful order arise within the context of an activity immoral on the whole? If war is totally right and the means to its success are self-justifying, or if war is totally wrong and not ever to be justified on moral grounds, then responsibility within the chain of command to distinguish between lawful and unlawful orders, between justifiable and unjustifiable conduct in war, is rendered nugatory.

I would not presume to say that for the clarification of military justice and the future conduct of American men in arms we needed convictions in the Mylai cases. That was for the courts to decide. Still I suggest that the British may have accumulated a tradition of military justice which we do not have and sorely need. And I do say that from time to time conviction of violations may be needed if a decisive imprint is to be made upon those who hold views on the political right with its indiscriminate opinion of the *morality* of war or upon those who hold views on the political left and upon the average citizen who alike hold indiscriminate opinions of the *immorality* of war as a state action.

The second thing worth remarking on in Calley's testimony is the fact that he could not bring himself to say he had "killed" anyone. Instead, the acceptable words to him were the inherently more indiscriminate terms "destroy" and "waste 'em." How could such a young man be produced by the American community and then by the military? I suggest that the fundamental explanation is not to be found in military experience, as much as military men may need the imposition of limits to which they are unaccustomed. The basic flaw is rather that in the American moral ethos "killing" is falsely and misleadingly taken to be always wrong. In this, the commandment "Thou shalt not kill" is entirely misunderstood. It always meant "Thou shalt do no murder," no unlawful killing. Therefore, the commandment entails what Lt. Calley said he never heard of, i.e., a just distinction between lawful and unlawful orders, a distinction between murder and killing in war.

The last thing that we should say is that military

indoctrination failed Lt. Calley. The first failure was that of church and local communities and institutions; it was dereliction on the part of leaders of domestic opinion and academic political analysts who generally engage in riotous moralizing, so far as this may have reached Calley or any of our men in arms. The same moral malaise in our modern culture produced a president who, while trying to extricate us responsibly from a war now deemed wrong, needed to say that Vietnam may be "the last war"! How sick unto death this nation is can be measured by the number of "hawks" and "doves" who alike agree with Lt. Calley that there is no just line to be drawn between good and bad killings in war or in *this* war. We should all believe (since we should believe the best of everyone) that Lt. Calley spoke the truth when he said he never "wantonly" killed a human being in his entire life, if there is no objective way to distinguish indiscriminate from legitimate killing in war. From right and from left, the American people seem resolved to conclude that the Vietnam war abolishes that distinction on which civilization very much depends.

*　　*　　*

Another question is often asked: Under what circumstances is the state justified in using military force beyond its borders? That, it seems to me, is a strange question, since in any proper meaning of the word a state is always "using" military force beyond its borders. In season and out of season, the state uses its monopoly of superior force *ad intra* to deter violation of law and to sustain the customary adherence of its people to agreed laws, even when it is not overtly arresting or punishing violators. By contrast with that, no state possesses a *monopoly* of power *ad extra:* that was the enduring verdict at Babel. Each acts with other states according to the law of move and countermove. But this means the state will always be "using" its military force beyond its borders—where else?—in the interstate system, i.e., using its force in season and out of season as a (major or minor) component of its influence and power of action in that system. In this broad but actual and uninterrupted sense of "use," a nation is not only allowed to use force beyond its borders; it is condemned to do so under the verdict at Babel. It can easily be seen that this is a blessing according to the mandate of the Noachan covenant with mankind by which power can only be limited by further and countervailing power. For this reason there are no "wandering" nations—nations which, like our father Abraham, go by faith forth into a far country seeking a good they know not of. That is the business of the "people of God," of the synagogue and the church in all ages; it is improper to states, even as a direct political vocation is improper to churches.

Thus, an Israel of the spirit may seek the reconciliation of mankind in some distant city. But, the Israel of the flesh cannot, I judge, abide a peace without a security position at Sharm el Sheik, nor can Israel in the interstate system abandon the Golan Heights to a potentially hostile power. Israel needs self-executing positions, not alliances or "guarantees" only. She will not simply yield to the novel dictum that after victory in war a state should return to the same insecure boundaries as a condition of peace. Moreover, the present generation of statesmen in Israel need to destine and enable their countrymen in years to come (whatever may be their idle "wouldings") to defend boundaries that will more surely protect that state's vital interests.

Unless, that is, Israel is forced to accept something other, by the impingement upon her of many encountering powers, allied and opposed, major and minor, with their never congruent interests. If justice does not lie, at least institutions are wrought, in the jar of these circumstances. Perhaps some approximation to a self-executing protective policy can be worked out without sovereign Israeli presence—a closer approximation than former international understandings that Suez should be open to the traffic of all nations, that a powerful maritime ally might have an interest in sending a ship through the blockaded straits of Tiran, or that that same ally in urging a cease fire could be counted on to prevent further increase of Soviet power in the Middle East while the cease fire was in effect. To be present at political creation in that part of the world clearly requires the framing of a use of power beyond borders arranged in such a way that Israel herself will be effectively present if not geographically present in the execution of the guarantees; or else other powers must be bound to execute them by some contrivance that is more reliable than present resolution, good intentions, promises, or changeable allied national interests. Other powers must be *made* to have an interest in the execution of guarantees approximating to that of Israeli geography, if it is true to say that geography is not an important part of that nation's security.

Having established the justification for the use of force beyond one's boundaries, let us take the question one step further and determine whether armed support of revolution or opposition to revolution in other countries is ever justifiable. The question is a most difficult one, for it asks about a *specific* use of force beyond one's borders: intervening in the affairs of another state to either instigate, support, or help repress armed revolution within that state. To give an answer requires that a decision first be made about the priority to be given to the objective of establishing and preserving a world order based on the principle of nonintervention. While the ideal of a global government of a world community is a pre-Babel paradise-notion, an unearthly, unhistorical, and finally—thank God!—a forbidden objective, the ideal of a system of noninterventionary multiple states is not. That may be a remote, unlikely goal. If achieved, it would be a stability ever threatening to break down. Still, the idea of a global multistate system based on overriding importance assigned to the proscription of armed intervention in the affairs of other states is a possibly highest, direct objective of interstate politics. That could be (in Maritain's words) a historically possible ideal.

One thing, however, has to be said: if we want to establish or preserve a noninterventionary system, it has to be remembered that no interstate system works automatically. A noninterventionary system must rest upon noninterventionary *policy*—governing the *abstentions* of states, governing also the *readiness* of states to *punish violations* of that principle, and all the while governing the *"use"* of power beyond one's own border in the form of credible possible enforcements that would be more unacceptable than anything to be gained by intervention in behalf of or against revolutionary causes. Thus, in the multistate system, nonintervention as a historically possible ideal requires at least this one exception, namely, the implied right to intervene to bring protective retribution upon any violation of that policy, to impel compliance, to deter future noncompliance. In interstate politics there are no self-enforcing or self-fulfilling policies. While, in ideal, nonintervention depends (like any rule or law) largely upon the compliance, the abstentions of the parties concerned, still in the last resort active sanctions or interventions to compel observance would be needed, whether the source of the enforcing action is a powerful member state or the agency of a regional collectivity of states. There must be not only compliance but compulsion to comply, and there must be deterrence of noncompliance.

One may think it odd that a policy of nonintervention must still, in some form or measure, count on potential or actual intervention for the policy to become effectual among the encountering powers. Whoever thinks so wishes in vain to abrogate the perduring Noachan covenant with mankind establishing government and placing in its hands fit instruments. Just so, one may speak of a coalition government where the constraints are present and remain intact in the general order and acquiescence of a people and the parties in power agree and are able *to govern;* but the "coalition government" in Laos hardly qualifies as one. Or—to give an additional example—the International Control Commission established in Indo-China by the Geneva Conference was never in any way capable of being an instrument of *government* to hold human destructiveness at bay. Like the Holy Roman Empire, it was a contradiction in each of its three terms.

Still the ideal of a global system of nonintervening states remains a historical possibility. All we would have to do would be to choose this as the top interstate political priority, a notch higher than we judged revolutionary or counterrevolutionary justice to be desirable domestically in another state, or to be causes to be effected or assisted by armed intervention by us in any other state. All we would have to be willing to resist by force is revolutionary or counterrevolutionary justice when these, however radical domestically, threatened to become interventionary, this way or that, in some other state. Then an interstate policy of nonintervention might be made to work. Let us call that not-impossible, historical ideal Scylla: a very safe world, but, I suspect, a dead world as well.

Therefore, a world order of states impelled not to intervene with arms in the affairs of any other state should not, perhaps, be given topmost priority. It is, indeed, difficult to argue that *justice* should not be the principal objective in interstate politics. However, if justice is taken to be the highest goal in the struggle for positions of power not only within domestic political life but in the interstate system as well, then *just aggressive* wars become possible and desirable on every side—the just aggressive wars that were plainly the reasonable entailment of the "just war" theory throughout the centuries before the destructiveness of warfare became so great as to be thought disproportionate to the good to be gained by advancing the cause of justice through resort to arms across (or beneath) borders. For this reason Pontifical teachings in recent decades have pronounced that wars of aggression can never today be rightfully initiated, however just the cause. If this verdict should be overturned, then a world order of noninterventionary states is not the highest historical ideal, although it is not an impossible objective. Instead, justice would take precedence to warrant the use of arms beyond one's own borders in interstate politics. Just wars of liberation against long-established evils would again become morally admissible: against South Africa, or Portuguese Africa; of North Vietnamese to liberate the South, and South Vietnamese to liberate the North; to liberate the French Canadians or the Eskimos in Alaska. Let us call this not-impossible historical ideal Charybdis.

*   *   *

Today, ships of state sail between this Charybdis and that Scylla, between the claims of justice and the need for order. Through this narrow defile we must seek the answer to the final question: What are the prospects for peaceful change in the direction of greater justice and security among states? Nuclear means of destruction have not essentially changed the requirement of order and the claims of justice in the political life of mankind. The prospects for peaceful change in the direction of greater justice and security among states depend on the priority assigned to one or the other of these objectives in interstate politics, on whether we say that greater justice must be achieved even by interventionary political violence before there can be stability or whether we say that the destructiveness of modern war is so great that justice is driven to seek actualization by other means. There is *not* going to be agreement on one of these propositions to the exclusion of the other. The prospects for peaceful change toward greater justice and security among states depend, therefore, upon our capacity for new political creation under the pressure of the nuclear threat. The danger is that we will continue simply to be immobilized (the proponents of justice and the proponents of order each accusing the other) while outstanding problems and unresolved disputes accumulate.

Order is not a higher value in politics than justice, but neither is justice a higher value than order. Both are in some respects conditional to the other. Order is a means to justice, but also justice is a means of securing order. Order is for the sake of justice, since the only real political justice is an ordered justice; yet justice is no less for the sake of order, since the only real political order in which men may dwell in community and peace is one that is just enough to command the love and allegiance of men, or at least their acquiescence and their compliance. Order and justice are ever in tension yet in interrelation;

and both are terminal goals in politics' act of being *proper* politics (its *bene esse*).

Still there is asymmetry between these values, and we know that men will choose tyranny over anarchy (which permits no ordered life at all). We must attend to the preservation of an ordered polity and an orderly inter-state system so that there can be the conditions for improving the justice actualized among men and between states.

Yet, proponents of the primacy of justice and propo-nents of the primacy of order, in and for itself and insofar as each conditions the other, alike have a good case in interstate politics. Claimants for justice and claimants for order are each correct in what they affirm, wrong only in their denial of the importance of the other objective. The nuclear threat has changed essentially nothing in the nature of these political options. The sad fact is that the pressures of the nuclear age provoke each side in this perennial political dispute to greater animus in accusing the other of willingness to bring the house down. From this there is no probability that we will come together in a new moment of political creation. The prospects for peaceful change in the direction of greater justice and security among states altogether depend upon the ability of the claimants of justice and the ability of the claimants of order to cast out the beam from their own eyes and to quit seeing only the mote in the eye of the other—to cease faulting the other, at least equally correct political analysis. Perhaps in retrospect it could be said that the nuclear threat to all mankind had slightly to do with bringing to pass this accomplishment. But the main source will be worldly works of political creation that should anyway have been done to call into being contrivances across which a greater identification of collective man with collective man may pass. Such political creation is only obstructed by those who place truth and beauty, goodness and piety behind one of these objectives only. The higher works of justice ought to be done, but the lesser works of ordering power ought never to be left undone.

IV. VIETNAM AND AMERICAN VALUES

Mark O. Hatfield

The role of values in international politics is not being considered seriously enough by those who plan and implement our foreign policy. Moral factors have received superficial attention by the social scientists who seem dominated by behavioral, quantitative, statistical, approaches to all our problems. A characteristic of the age appears to be that we are able to find significant answers to insignificant questions; that the only things that count are the things that can be counted. Our government officials can efficiently systematize world crises into memoranda prepared by Inter-Departmental Working Groups, analyzed by Senior Review Groups, and presented to the Chief Executive with all the options thus nearly insuring that he will select the prudent, middle course. But we have not found the way to ask whether our actions are right or wrong. Values, ethics, morality, compassion, do not make convenient "inputs" into our security planning process. But we as a people must examine our moral responsibilities, unless we are to believe that international politics are beyond the moral judgment of the nation's citizens.

While questions about morality and international politics are right to ask, there has been too much verbal overkill both by those who defend and those who attack the policies of our government. We have become tired of talking about our plight, and we are unmoved by intellectual discourse and clever rhetoric. I find it hard to talk about "morality" in an impersonal and intellectual way. Morality and values must be more than lofty nebulous concepts; they must come from the depths of one's own experience, from the convictions, faith, and commitments of one's own life. So I cannot address these questions and merely offer impersonal, intellectual ideas. I must reveal something of myself.

Fundamentally, I believe in the ultimate worth and value of every individual human life. This is universal in scope; it applies to all men. The lives of all Vietnamese, living in North or South Vietnam, are as priceless as the lives of Americans. There is no difference between the value of a Chinese peasant or an English Member of Parliament. I feel impelled by an imperative of love and compassion for my fellow man. This sense of responsibility toward fellow human beings means I want each person on this earth to have at least the minimum necessary to sustain and nurture human life. This involves a commitment to alleviate suffering and provide a hope for a decent future for every man. Such responsibility must be grounded in simple human love and acceptance of others. For me, these are not casual opinions, but deep convictions. I believe every man is of infinite value because he is the creation of God. Race, position, nationality, and ideology are all transcended by God's compassion, and mankind is seen and loved as one. So if I discover my personal identity in this love, then I must strive to act in service toward all others.

What is the relevance of my personal ethics to the foreign policy of the U.S. government? The traditional "realist" position has maintained that we cannot use naive individualistic notions of "morality" to govern a state's relations toward other states. Though an individual is capable of moral judgments and actions, the same principles do not apply to states. Though an individual can act in a self-giving way, a nation always acts in its own "national interest" pursuing its security according to the realist position. This is its obligation to its own citizens. Further, the realist position holds that as nations prudently seek their own interests, a balance between them will occur, creating stability and perhaps relative justice.

This approach, however, provides the nation with a certain immunity from moral judgment. When values regarding relations among men are viewed as irrelevant to relations among states, the danger is that one can justify a national moral abdication. In the *Psychology of Power*, R. V. Sampson eloquently pointed out the logical consequences of fully embracing the realist perspective:

> Already the apologists of "realism" are busy exhorting us to accept the realities of life in the atomic age, and learn to live with the Bomb. According to these theorists—and they are to be found high in the councils of Church and State—we have never been so secure as we are today under the umbrella of the Bomb. The terror inspired by the equilibrium of fear is such that we can rely on the Bomb as an effective deterrent, a super-policeman guaranteeing the peace of mankind. In other words, the peace which man has been unable to gain through two millennia of the advocacy of brotherly love will now be secured through fear. What we failed to win under the symbol of the star of Bethlehem, we shall gain under the symbol of the mushroom cloud. Men will not act rationally from love, but they will learn to do so from fear. In fact, the atomic age has at last "proved" what so many men have always wanted to believe in their hearts: that the doctrine of the carpenter of Nazareth is a monumental irrelevance; that his sacrifice on Calvary was pathetic, noble perhaps, but futile and pointless. For this is the logic of the maintenance of peace through the deterrent.[1]

I have come to believe that it is invalid to separate completely individual and corporate moral judgment. We must attempt to apply the moral principles that govern person-to-person relations to groups of people and nations. We must discover how moral values and ethical

[1] Ronald V. Sampson, *The Psychology of Power* (New York: Random House, 1966), p. 181.

ideals can influence and mold our nation's actions toward other states and peoples.

As a culture we profess values and ideals molded by our Judaeo-Christian heritage. These focus on the importance and worth of the individual human life. Our Declaration of Independence declares that *all* men are created equal and are endowed by their creator with certain inalienable rights. Though these values have not been totally fulfilled within our society, they still remain as the ideals that characterize our political ideology and have won our conceptional allegiance. And they should govern our foreign policy. Yet, in the "realistic" pursuit of our national interest, they have been often fundamentally ignored.

*   *   *

Let us consider the relevance of our values in light of our experience in Vietnam. Our blatant tendency to dismiss moral considerations in planning foreign policy is most clearly evident in the policy and conduct of this war. The Vietnam experience must teach us the dangers of assuming that our nation is immune from moral judgments and considerations as it pursues its presumed interests. The basic question about Vietnam today is not one of strategy or diplomacy, but a moral question. All those realists who argue that moral concerns, divorced from assessments of our own interests, have little role in guiding our foreign policy must account for the moral travesty that has occurred in Vietnam and explain whether and how their position could have prevented it.

The degradation of our values in Vietnam becomes apparent when we first recognize the scope of the destructive military force we have applied there. The ratio of our fire power (the total amount of explosives we have used in Indo-China) compared to that of the enemy has been estimated to be as high as *500* to 1.[2] Since the beginning of our involvement in Indo-China, the United States has expended over 10 million tons of explosives, more than the total used in World War II.[3] Therefore, we must confront the grim reality that we are responsible for most of the destruction, casualties, and death in Indo-China. What have been the human costs of this war? We can estimate that over 300,000 civilians have been killed; and there have been probably 1 million civilian casualties. According to official figures, 926,000 Vietnamese soldiers have been killed—this includes 141,392 South Vietnamese soldiers and 784,762 North Vietnamese and Vietcong. Over 55,000 Americans have died.[4] As many as 6 million refugees have been created in Vietnam since 1964. Another 1.5 million refugees have been created in Cambodia, and about 750,000 in Laos.[5] To gain some perspective, we can compare this death toll to Hiroshima and Nagasaki, where a total of about 115,000 were killed.

Then consider the whole policy of the "body count" we have used as an indication of military "progress." This directly implies that our strategy is based on achieving success through destroying enough lives. The logic of this mentality is that we have been willing to obliterate those who oppose our presence and policy, with little or no regard for the human costs that are exacted, nor for the

[2] Figures from Office of Assistant Secretary of Defense (Public Affairs Division, January 15, 1970), cited in *Indochina 1971, White Paper for Peace in Southeast Asia* (Philadelphia: American Friends Service Committee, 1970), p. 4.

[3] *Ibid.,* p. 14.

[4] U.S. Department of Defense, Office of Assistant Secretary of Defense (Public Affairs), News Release, December 2, 1971.

[5] *Refugee And Civilian War Casualty Problems In Indochina,* a staff report prepared for the use of the Subcommittee to Investigate Problems Connected With Refugees And Escapees of the Committee on the Judiciary, United States Senate (Washington, D.C.: Government Printing Office, September 28, 1970).

innocent who are sent to death. Vietnamization only further highlights the moral impoverishment of our policy, for now it is assumed that our presence and actions in Vietnam will be acceptable if fewer Americans, although more Asian, lives are lost in the implementation of our policy. Thus, it appears that Asian lives are held to be of less worth than American. Consider, for example, the invasion into Laos in 1971, totally planned and operated by the U.S. command. Over 150,000 U.S. air sorties were flown in support of this operation. Yet, it was considered more "tolerable" because only 127 Americans died, and no U.S. "ground combat troops" were used in Laos, although at least 1,500 South Vietnamese and an alleged 13,000 North Vietnamese and Vietcong lost their lives. One troubling feature of the "Nixon Doctrine" is that it can result in paying "allies" to fight and die in our wars, for our policies, and with our support in dollars and air power, but not lives.

We have assumed that our might will make right, and regarded ourselves as above the law, beyond judgment. A sense of national self-righteousness has prevented us from confronting the dark side of our national soul. Our actions in Vietnam have made a mockery of our professed moral values and ideals. Further, my individual moral values, as a citizen and a human, are totally in opposition to those actions. This is a personal judgment which each person must honestly confront. It goes far deeper than having mere opinions about policy, for it involves determining who we are as persons and what values and principles demand our allegiance.

We must recognize that actions claimed to be in the national interest can be an utter refutation of the ideas and values that give us our identity as a nation. Such a contradiction is unnecessary and it can destroy our national integrity. Preserving our integrity and our identity as a humane, compassionate society must be our foremost aim. Our national interest must never be allowed to subvert our national integrity.

*　　*　　*

Our experience in Vietnam is one reason for us to reapply moral values to our thinking about international relations. Another is the revolutionary changes sweeping the world. The cleavage between the affluent and the impoverished is the salient division in the world today. This is not an ideological distinction, between the "Communist Bloc" and the "Free World," but an economic one, between the rich and the poor.

The per capita Gross National Product for North America, Western Europe, Australia, and New Zealand is $2,920. The United States alone controls about 40 percent of the world's total economic wealth, although it has only 6 percent of the world's population. The per capita Gross National Product for Latin America is $440; for the Near East it is $360; in Africa it is $175; for East Asia, excluding Japan, it is $160; and in South Asia it is $90.

The crux of the problem is population growth. The economies of impoverished nations are not expanding rapidly enough to meet their expanding populations. Further, what economic expansion does take place usually fails to affect the lot of the common man. Two thirds of humanity lives in developing countries; their members are increasing at between 2.5 and 3 percent per year, compared to a 1 percent growth in U.S. population.

This has led to a serious unemployment crisis in the developing world. The size of the labor force is growing far more rapidly than the economies of poorer nations. India, for instance, adds 100,000 people to its labor force *each week*. During the 1970s, in the non-Communist developing world, about 170 million additional people will be added to the labor force. This growth will be 50 percent higher than in the 1960s. During that decade, unemployment grew despite economic growth. But in this decade, the growth of the labor force, and the consequent unemployment will be far greater.

Population growth also accentuates the nutritional and health needs of the poorer countries. Malnutrition and starvation still persist despite the "Green Revolution." When we compare the number of people per physician, we find that in the United States there are 670 persons per doctor. But in South Vietnam, there are 37,430 people per doctor. In Nigeria, the ratio is 44,230 to 1; in Saudi Arabia, 13,000 to 1; in Nepal, 41,180 to 1; and in Ethiopia, 68,520 to 1.

The disparity between the affluent and the impoverished presents the greatest threat to peace. It spawns the greatest potential for violence. There will be no true peace unless human needs are met.

What is the relevance of moral values to these conditions? And why should a rich country, such as the United States, attempt to help the world's disadvantaged? Should we do so just because it may be in our interest? I believe not. For if that is our only motivation, a self-defeating paternalism will continue to afflict all our efforts. We will want nations to do things our way, using our methods, buying our goods, and accepting our values. Today, the impoverished countries are decisively rejecting such an approach. We must do whatever is possible to assist the people of the world simply because it is right. We need essentially moral convictions and motivation. We must see any man's suffering as the responsibility of all men and make a commitment to the enhancement of human life because we believe every life is of value.

Rethinking the role of moral values in relations between states is also necessary because of the great advances in modern weapons. Consider the expansion of our nuclear arsenals. It is estimated that the United States and the Soviet Union together possess the equivalent explosive power of 15 tons of TNT for each person in the world. Yet, newer weapons systems continue to develop. Technology itself, when not controlled by other factors, does not lead to strategic stability but to instability, and the continuation of the arms race. With each addition to our arsenal and each new weapons system, the chance of a nuclear accident is that much greater. Therefore, it seems to me that moral arguments justify taking "risks" to stop the arms race. Ultimately, we cannot achieve the true well-being and welfare of mankind through the reliance on fear—through the balance of terror. We currently devote billions of dollars, and thousands of our brightest citizens, to perfecting the redundant and often needless intricacies of our strategic nuclear deterrent force. What we need is a similar commitment to move beyond the force of fear.

A primary distinguishing feature of the modern era is the revolution in mankind's awareness and consciousness. The communications revolution, with the impact of radio, TV, and movies, has given a greater portion of mankind a sense of participation in one world. This growing consciousness transcends ideological and national boundaries. This process also has a dramatic effect on the role of values in international affairs. As people find their identity in ways that transcend the boundaries of nations, they will be less prone to support narrow national aims. The greater recognition of what mankind has in common will increase the longing for peace. President Eisenhower touched on this theme in August of 1959 when he said, "People want peace so much that one of these days governments had better get out of their way and let them have it." [6]

There is a growing gap between the consciousness of people and the policies of their governments. We cannot assume that the values and presuppositions that supported foreign policy stances in the immediate postwar era are adequate today. The United States has made no fundamental change in our foreign policy in the postwar era. We still see the military containment of communism throughout the world as the chief determinant of foreign policy. Yet, there have been deep changes in the awareness and outlook of people in the past twenty five years. Europeans, for instance, and many Americans no longer see Western Europe as about to be run over by Soviet armies. There are rapidly changing political attitudes toward East-West relations in Europe. Yet, our policy and strategy has not been significantly altered; about 26 billion of 79 billion defense dollars of the United States are devoted toward the defense of Europe against conventional Soviet military invasion. Our fundamental presuppositions about our policy there are still regarded as sacrosanct and rarely questioned.

As political consciousness grows in the Third World, people there also fail to see the major issues as the ideology and politics of the Communist versus the Free World. Rather, they are searching for the best ways to promote economic, social, and political development, regardless of what labels or names may be attached to it. Yet, U.S. policy, treaty commitments, and objectives are based, first of all, upon ideological competition, rather than upon desire to meet the needs of the people in these countries. We assume that others see the world as we do.

[6] Dwight D. Eisenhower in London radio broadcast with Prime Minister Macmillan: *Public Papers of the President* (Washington, D.C.: Government Printing Office, 1960), p. 625.

Far too often, the result is that we support unrepresenta-
tive regimes whose outlook fails to reflect the growing
political awareness within their countries and whose
policies are not dedicated to the welfare of their people.

Growing political awareness and consciousness, then,
stimulated by communications and technology, is rendering present assumptions of foreign policy obsolete. In the
future, the disparity between people's desires and hopes,
and their government's policies, is likely to grow. The
bonds of mankind are transcending the barriers of
ideology. It is incumbent upon us to respond to this
growing new global awareness with an outlook inspired
by new values that proclaim the unity and commonality
of mankind.

In summary, there are these fundamental changes
taking place in our modern world: the increasing disparity between rich and poor; the greater threat from
destructive weapons; and the growth in political and
social consciousness. Combined, all these necessitate the
reapplication of moral values in the future conduct of
international relations.

*　　　*　　　*

Having maintained that we must creatively reapply
moral values to thinking about international relations, we
must now examine how these values may relate to the use
of military force. In so doing, however, we should
consider not just those situations when force would be
actively utilized, but the actual presence of our force
throughout the world. We have about 332 major overseas
military bases and about 3,000 other property holdings
and defense facilities. About 900,000 troops are stationed away from our shores; in fact, more U.S. troops
are stationed outside the country than all the troops of

all the other world's armies deployed outside their borders. Our enemies in Europe see U.S. troops on their borders; our Asian enemies see U.S. ships sailing off their coast and U.S. bases in countries around their borders. In addition, our military assistance program supplies arms to 47 countries. Next year's military aid budget is approximately $1.6 billion. In the past, the United States has provided about 50 percent of all military supplies to developing countries; Russia has supplied about 20 percent; and Britain and France most of the remainder.

The changes in the world and the necessity to integrate moral values into our policy formulation require us to rethink totally our judgments about the use of military force. We must reconsider the likely consequences of our use of military power. First, in any situation, there is the threat of widespread destruction. Any direct application of force by the United States has an enormous potential to escalate. Once military force is introduced, it becomes hard to contain and tends to generate momentum that is difficult, almost impossible, to reverse.

Second, we must recognize that military force is often not likely to solve the fundamental problems at the roots of any conflict. The plight of the impoverished countries hardly will be solved by weapons and soldiers. Using our military aid, for instance, to maintain various regimes, particularly status quo regimes, is no way to serve the needs of the people or remove the root sources of conflict. Force can be used to counter or deter the use of force by an adversary; but it will be just as likely to accentuate the root sources of conflict than to permanently resolve conflict situations.

Third, in today's world, the use of our military force may be to the liking of a particular regime, but it can easily be used against the will of their people. The gap between leaders of governments and the attitudes of their citizens means that the requests of other regimes that may be threatened can never alone be sufficient grounds to justify our use of military force.

The whole question of the role and effectiveness of military power in resolving conflicts can be seen in light of our experience in Asia. In our defense budget each year in the past, a certain portion has been earmarked for conventional forces to be available for an "Asian contingency." Now the expenditures we have made over the past ten years in preparation for a major war, presumably with China, in Asia, total about $180 billion. None of that includes the money we have spent in Vietnam, which has been in addition to our normal force structure. Our Vietnam expenditures during the last ten years, conservatively estimated, would total at least another $100 billion. Therefore, in the past decade, we have spent at least $280 billion dollars for the posturing, preparation, and actual use of our military forces in Asia. Has this investment increased or decreased the violence there? Has it dealt with the root cause of turmoil, unrest, and conflict? Has it increased or decreased the possibilities of future peace in Asia?

During the past ten years, the problems of overpopulation, unemployment, malnutrition, and poverty have all grown, breeding unrest and instability throughout the countries of Asia. During this time, our total expenditures for nonmilitary assistance to the countries of Asia, such as AID projects and other social and economic assistance, have totaled about $5 billion dollars—$280 billion versus $5 billion!

I am not suggesting that we should merely abandon our military posture in Asia, or that such a posture has not, in times past, made some positive contributions of deterrence. But I do believe that such a massive commitment to the presence and use of military force in Asia during the past decade has neither eased the potential for conflict there nor led us any closer to peace.

Rather, violence and political instability have characterized Asia's past decade; despite our purposes and motives, history will show that our own military force bears at least a measure of the responsibility for creating and intensifying those conditions.

As we look to Asia's future, our past investment and over-reliance on our military power seems all the more imprudent. The underlying problems of Asian society are nowhere near solution, and they seem quite likely to breed continued turbulence and conflict in the future. Some protest that these problems are insoluble. Yet, one cannot help but wonder what Asia's destiny might be if we had made just a small portion of the commitment, in terms of money and effort, to alleviating the social and economic plight of this region that we made to insuring our military hegemony over it.

The review of our use of force during the past decade in Asia should at least create new questions about when we are justified in using military force beyond our borders. The concept of conventional deterrence seems sound and defendable in theory. Yet, we must analyze what in reality we have condoned in the name of that policy. We must go beyond the intentions of our policy to discover whether the effect, in some cases, has been to promulgate conflict rather than deter it. And we must ask whether our commitment to conventional military deterrence has succeeded in creating political stability, or whether it has become an obsession that has fostered a neglect of the social and economic causes of political instability.

Thus, we can see how the thoughtless use of military force can become counterproductive and place us in direct contradiction with our moral values. But the question remains as to whether and when a nation is justified in using force to achieve various ends.

Most would maintain, and I would agree, that a nation's use of force is justified when the survival and identity of that nation, and the integrity of institutions and ideals, are directly threatened by the military actions of an adversary. It is difficult to be more specific without considering actual examples or hypothetical situations. Suffice it to say that if and when such a direct threat would present itself to our nation, a consensus of the people will recognize it as such. Likewise, they will find it hard to believe, and rightly so, that the internal political turmoil of those countries halfway around the globe have anything to do with such a threat. Ironically, the greatest threat to the integrity of our institutions and ideals as a nation during the postwar era has come because of our involvement in Indo-China. The erosion of our constitutional principles, the purposeful deception by national leaders, and the massive disillusionment of Americans with their government have all been created by our involvement in Indo-China. Thus, the reckless and excessive use of military power can devastate the very ideals it purports to defend.

The way much of our military power is deployed and utilized has lost any sensible relationship to insuring our security and preserving our ideals and institutions. Of course, it is argued that much of our potential use of force is tied to alliances with other nations. We have come to believe that the survival of particular regimes in other countries has a relationship to our own security, and this formed the basis of postwar alliances. But an examination of those alliances shows that, almost without exception, they are being questioned by member governments and challenged from within by growing numbers of citizens in these countries. Furthermore, on the major occasions when our military force has actually been applied in recent years, in Vietnam, for example, and in the Dominican Republic, it has been done unilaterally; we then have attempted to create the appearance of some "allied" support, after the fact. Much of our alliance structure has lost touch with the political realities in other countries. Often, it has become more of a means for imposing our independent judgments about our interests on nations whose regimes calculate they can best preserve their power by securing the rewards we offer them.

All this suggests that we cannot assume that our alliance structure, as it presently exists, accurately reflects the will of the people in these countries, and therefore justifies the deployment and application of our military power in its defense. Of course we have many true allies. But we can no longer glibly assume that our force is welcomed by the people whose governments, on paper, are our allies.

Unless the most direct and imminent threat to our survival is clear to a majority of the people, I believe the *unilateral* use of military force by our government is most difficult to justify. That includes the cases where we obtain the thin trapping of allied support for actions that are, in effect, unilateral. Such unilateral judgment implies a kind of national self-righteousness and that we know what is best for the nations of the world. This can lead us again to the assumption that our might can make us right.

If force is to be used outside of our borders, it seems to be almost essential that it be in response to a genuine multilateral mandate from a wide consensus of nations; further, it must be a consensus reflecting not merely the wish of other governments, but the will of their citizens.

The United Nations provides one vehicle for reaching such a consensus, although its structure and decision-making process present some practical problems. Other forums for international judgment, both formal and informal, might be found or created. But discovering the proper formal means is not nearly as important as accepting the principle that our use of force beyond our borders can be justified only as part of a genuine, multilateral judgment and mandate. Only grave, direct, and imminent threats to our identity and survival should justify the use of appropriate defensive, unilateral military force. It must be admitted that situations where our nation's actual survival is threatened by a conventional military invasion seem quite improbable.

The most common use of our military force today is to assist governments in putting down and preventing revolutions. The truth is that the United States is increasingly seen throughout the world as a status quo, counterrevolutionary force. Our policy of intervention in revolutions is usually counterproductive, and morally questionable. Revolutions have their own internal dynamic. A government not meeting the needs of its country will never be secure from opposition and should not be defended by the United States. Revolutions most always are born out of social conditions of unemployment, poverty, and hopelessness. Our attempts to thwart such revolutions are usually seen as attempts to thwart change in those countries, and we appear insensitive to the needs of the people and concerned only for our national interests. When this is the case, such intervention again conflicts with certain of our own values and ideals.

Many people forget that the United States has a tradition of support for revolutionary movements. Our nation was born out of revolution, and many of our past presidents have affirmed the rights of a people to throw off oppressive governments. For much of our history we applauded revolutionary ideas and causes throughout the world. But since World War II we have come mistakenly to identify *all* revolutionary ferment as the product of monolithic communism. This attitude has separated us from our own heritage and prevented our understanding the roots of revolutions.

There may well be situations today where revolutions will become inevitable, because evolution has been impossible. In such an event, there is no reason why we must regard every revolution as anathema. (Of course, any revolutionary change is not necessarily change for the better.) In fact, we could even consider giving rhetorical support, in principle, to certain revolutionary pressures. We should candidly acknowledge that the world is being remolded by revolutionary changes and that governments must either adapt or become the eventual victims of the dynamics of such change.

The entire meaning of "national security" must be reexamined if we are to take seriously the perspectives that have been previously presented. Most Americans would maintain that we should use force beyond our borders and intervene in revolutions when our national security is threatened. But the real issue is that we must redefine and clarify what we mean by "national security." Security should mean the survival and the continued existence of the nation and its fundamental social and political institutions. Where are the threats to that security? Are they from an invading foreign army? From revolutions abroad? Or do they come from within, from unresponsive, archaic machinery of government; from estranged, disenfranchised citizens who insist that the "system" does not work; from racial strife and antagonism; and from deteriorating, hopeless cities and their embittered, impoverished citizens? These are far more direct "threats" to our security. Yet, such conditions persist, in part, because of the billions spent to protect against supposed "security threats" in distant lands.

Where has our present understanding of "security" led us? It has given us the Vietnam war. It has created an enormous, expanding defense budget. It has wedded us to the doctrine of nuclear overkill. It has massively deployed our troops throughout the world. And at home we see unmet needs, internal strife, economic instability, and the estrangement of our younger generation. Have we found security? Or has our present strategy for achieving security made us only more insecure?

In redefining "national security," we must come to realize that justice and trust are essential to true security and peace. Deterrence, and the balance of power, is an interim strategy which offers no certain and lasting hope of peace. Fear and might will never be adequate to insure "security"; our military might can never be the *ultimate* guarantee of our safety. A true search for security must attempt to build trust in relations between nations, to assure that justice is sought, and to see that man's needs are fulfilled. One nation's trust can be strengthened and supported only by the response of another; this must be a mutual process. But at this point it seems that hardly anyone is even trying, hoping, or risking, and the state of perpetual insecurity continues. Our search for "security" must become a search for human fulfillment and well-being and for international trust. We can take the initiative toward these ends, creatively and hopefully exploring how goals we previously thought unattainable may be within the realm of the possible.

When we look at our destiny, and wonder what the prospects for peace and justice will be, we must remember that the world literally belongs to the young. Over half of the world's population is under twenty five, and three fourths of these young lives in developing countries.

In Latin America, for instance, one out of two persons is under eighteen. In Venezuela, 75 percent of the population is under thirty. All youth seem to be experiencing a universal cultural revolution. They exhibit new awareness, new hope, and new values. The young are now the majority and will shape our future.

Leaders of our world, however, are removed by generations from the majority of their citizens. Consider their ages: Brezhnev is sixty-four; Kosygin is sixty-seven; Mao is seventy-seven; Chiang Kai-shek is seventy-three; Sato is seventy; Pompidou is sixty-nine; Golda Meir is seventy-two; Franco is seventy-eight; and Haile Selassie is seventy-eight. When they depart, an era for their people may also come to a close. Our future will be determined, and can be radically reshaped, by new, fresh leadership responsive to the majority of youth in the world.

Finally, I want to conclude with some more personal thoughts about the inward search for outward peace. Self-analysis is always more difficult than either self-hatred or self-righteousness; that is just as true for a nation as it is for the individual. As a people, I believe we must try to understand what the Vietnam war has put us through and where we are going. This is not merely a corporate, impersonal exercise, but should involve individual, highly personal reflection for each of us. I am reminded of the words of Carl Jung, who wrote:

This war has pitilessly revealed to civilized man that he is still a barbarian, and has at the same time shown what an iron scourge lies in store for him if ever again he should be tempted to make his neighbor responsible for his own evil qualities. The psychology of the individual is reflected in the psychology of the nation. What the nation does is done also by each individual, and so long as the individual continues to do it, the nation will do likewise. Only a change in the attitude of the individual can initiate a change in the psychology of the Nation.[7]

[7] C. G. Jung, "Two Essays on Analytical Psychology," in *Collected Works,* vol. 7, p. 4, as quoted in Elizabeth O'Conner, *Our Many Selves* (New York: Harper & Row, 1971), p. 73.

Our nation's foremost need is the recovery of a relevant moral conscience. That must come ultimately through individuals. A nation's sense of morality always will be that of its people. We must find resources to fill the moral vacuum in American life and must begin by doing so in each of our lives. This can come through the rediscovery of our spiritual resources. In my own personal life, I have found that inner spiritual resources provide me with a concrete motive for concern for others, a source of resolute strength, and a basis for hope in the future.

The prospects for peace depend on us as individuals, as well as upon nations. They will depend upon whether we can discover the sources for inner strength and personal renewal, and whether we can establish in our own lives the basis for moral values that identify our individual destiny with the future of mankind.

SELECTED BIBLIOGRAPHY

Compiled by Ernest W. Lefever

Note: Though there is considerable literature on morality and warfare, there are relatively few books that deal explicitly with the relation of ethics to foreign policy or to international politics. All the titles listed below bear directly or indirectly on some facets of the problem of the relevance of Western ethical norms to the contingencies and necessities of international politics.

Acheson, Dean. "Morality, Moralism, and Diplomacy." *Yale Review,* 47 (Summer, 1958): 481-93.
————. *Power and Diplomacy.* Cambridge, Mass.: Harvard University Press, 1958.
Becker, Carl L. *The Heavenly City of the Eighteenth-Century Philosophers.* New Haven: Yale University Press, 1952.
Bennett, John C. *Foreign Policy in Christian Perspective.* New York: Charles Scribner's Sons, 1966.
Boorstin, Daniel J. *The Genius of American Politics.* Chicago: University of Chicago Press, 1953.
Booth, Alan. *Christianity and Power Politics.* New York: Association Press, 1961.
Brogan, D. W. *Politics in America.* New York: Harper & Bros., 1955.
Butterfield, Herbert. *International Conflict in the Twentieth Century—a Christian View.* New York: Harper & Bros., 1960.
Carr, E. H. *The Twenty Years' Crisis: 1919-1939.* 2nd ed. London: The Macmillan Co., 1946.

Collingwood, R. G. *The Idea of History*. London: Oxford University Press, 1946.

Davis, Harry R., and Robert C. Good (eds.). *Reinhold Niebuhr on Politics*. New York: Charles Scribner's Sons, 1960.

Dawson, Christopher H. *Beyond Politics*. New York: Sheed & Ward, 1939.

DeVisscher, Charles. *Theory and Reality in Public International Law*. Princeton: Princeton University Press, 1957.

Dulles, John Foster. "A Righteous Faith." *Life*, December 28, 1942, pp. 49-51.

——— .*War or Peace*. 2nd ed. New York: The Macmillan Co., 1957.

Eliot, T. S. *The Idea of a Christian Society*. New York: Harcourt, Brace & Co., 1949.

Falk, Richard A. *Law, Morality, and War in the Contemporary World*. New York: Frederick A. Praeger, 1963.

Finn, James (ed.). *Protest: Pacifism and Politics*. New York: Random House, 1967.

Fulbright, J. William. *The Arrogance of Power*. New York: Vintage Books, 1966.

Graebner, Norman A. *Ideas and Diplomacy: Readings in the Intellectual Tradition of American Foreign Policy*. Oxford: Oxford University Press, 1964.

Halle, Louis Joseph. *Choice for Survival*. New York: Harper & Bros., 1958.

Herz, John H. *Political Realism and Political Idealism*. Chicago: University of Chicago Press, 1951.

Hoffman, Stanley. *The State of War: Essays on the Theory and Practice of International Politics*. New York: Frederick A. Praeger, 1965.

Hunt, R. N. Carew. *The Theory and Practice of Communism*. New York: The Macmillan Co., 1952.